U^{TIM}nsworth

Articles from the
National Catholic Reporter

Written by Tim Unsworth

Chosen and Prefaced by Robert McClory

Foreword by Tom Roberts

Introduction by Jean Morman Unsworth

acta
PUBLICATIONS

TIM UNSWORTH
Articles from the National Catholic Reporter
Written by Tim Unsworth

Chosen and Prefaced by Robert McClory
Foreword by Tom Roberts
Introduction by Jean Morman Unsworth
Edited by Gregory F. Augustine Pierce
Cover and text design and typesetting by Patricia A. Lynch

Articles from the National Catholic Reporter are used with permission. All rights reserved.

Copyright © 2008 by ACTA Publications

Published by ACTA Publications, 5559 W. Howard Street, Skokie, IL 60077-2621, (800) 397-2282, www.actapublications.com

ISBN: 978-0-87946-366-3
Printed in the United States of America by Total Printing Systems
Year 15 14 13 12 11 10 09 08
Printing 15 14 13 12 11 10 9 8 7 6 5 4 3 2 First

U^{TIM}nsworth

Articles from the National Catholic Reporter

PUBLSHER'S NOTE

Tim Unsworth entered into his well-deserved eternal reward on April 30, 2008, the very day this book went to press. Of the great pain he suffered during his final illness, he joked, "Maybe I should have given more to the Propagation of the Faith."

ALSO BY TIM UNSWORTH

Here Comes Everybody: Stories of Church
(Crossroad Publishing Company, 1997

I Am Your Brother Joseph: Cardinal Bernardin of Chicago
(Crossroad Publishing Company, 1997)

Catholics on the Edge (Crossroad Publishing Company, 1995)

The Last Priests in America: Conversations with Remarkable Men
(Crossroad Publishing Company, 1991)

Lambs of Libertyville: A Working Community of Retarded Adults
(Contemporary Books, 1990)

With Jean Morman Unsworth
Upon This Rock: The Church, Work, Money and You
(ACTA Publications, 1991)

Contents

To Jean
pure and simple

Foreword

by Tom Roberts
Editor-at-large and News Director,
National Catholic Reporter

Even the most sophisticated among us are tugged along during the Triduum and Christmas observances by the pull of the story. Our early fascination with a babe in a manger and with a God nailed to a cross set the images from which we work for a lifetime, long before they mature into landscapes for deeper investigation and questions.

Stories are our "first contact with religion," writes Fr. Andrew Greeley in the introduction to *The Catholic Imagination*. It is in stories and in the imagination where religion begins.

It is safe to assume, I think, that as people of such rich stories we never stop craving for them to be made new in our midst, in our chapter of the long saga of this pilgrim people. Every age needs its storytellers. In modern U.S. Catholicism, Tim Unsworth was one of the best.

This little volume begins with a letter that has become its own story, part of the lore in which disparate elements seemed to match up flawlessly: in this case, a writer, a publication and a moment in time. It is easy to discern, looking back, that the letter, an open missive to the then-new archbishop of Chicago, Joseph Bernardin, contained a kind of writer's DNA that would point the way to Unsworth's success as a regular columnist for the *National Catholic Reporter* for twenty-five years. The letter began on a street corner amid a swirl of people, and involved food and riding the bus and walking and other everyday things that people do. It showed a fine eye for detail but never lost sight of the big picture. It was just funny enough in all the right places. And the letter was shot through with a robust affection for everyone and everything in those scenes that he painted—the deli, the cop on the corner, the dead priests, the live priests, the subway denizens, and all the nooks and crannies of the outsized church that served as the core of Tim's writer's observatory.

There's a timelessness, too, to his observations. These essays are a bit like the window the writer Sholom Aleichem provided into Judaism through the everyday stuff of the Jewish community: deeply human stories, in which the ordinary is mined for its great strength and humor and ability to illuminate a broader landscape...and all charged with a sense of the divine. So in the Catholic version, what was good advice in 1982 would be good advice today to most bishops: eat a sandwich in a deli; take a walk or a bus; move out of the mansion.

> What was good advice in 1982 would be good advice today to most bishops: eat a sandwich in a deli; take a walk or a bus; move out of the mansion.

Editors know that lots of people can have one moment of brilliance in which the ideas and the words all line up as they should. But the question is, will the dazzling rookie of spring be around at the end of the season? In a year or two or five? Usually the answer is no. It is devilishly difficult to write with such a deep humanity as Tim did, with so much humor and grace and wit. To do it consistently for a quarter of a century is, well, its own story.

The invitation, then, is to sink into a favorite chair, maybe with a good deli sandwich, and ramble with Tim beneath the shelter of his big-tent church, amid the saints and the sinners, the jokers and the giants. It's a place, as he once said of a parish he was writing about, where Christianity is seen "through a telescope, not a rearview mirror."

Introduction

by Jean Morman Unsworth

Tim Unsworth was always a writer. During his high school years, he had a sports column in the New Rochelle, New York, *Standard-Star*, as well as in the Iona Prep school newspaper. He was known as Dick, or "Unsie," then. His baptismal name is Richard, but having been called Tim, his religious name in the Christian Brothers of Ireland for almost 25 years, he chose to keep it when he left the Brothers in 1970 and he and I were married.

Working at De Paul University in alumni relations, Tim's writing skills were put to use, not only in grant writing but in speeches for everyone from the president of the university to members of the board of directors. But Tim's writing career took off in 1981 with a front-page blast in *NCR* following the death of Cardinal John Cody of Chicago. Here's how it happened. Tim and I were having a sandwich in Joe's Deli on Chicago Avenue and Rush Street when a Roman collar appeared in the take-out line. I recognized the Episcopal bishop from St. James Cathedral, and Tim and I laughed about the unlikelihood of a Roman Catholic bishop—much less a cardinal of the Church—ever waiting in line at a deli to buy his own sandwich. Two days later, Tim handed me a seven-page, single-spaced letter to the next archbishop, telling Joseph Bernardin that this was exactly what he should do. I said, "Tim, this is going to *NCR*." I mailed it that day.

A few days later, Michael Farrell, then the Opinion Editor of *NCR* called. I said, "Did you like his article?" Michael said, "Like it? We loved it! It's going on the front page this week." And that was the beginning of twenty-five years of Tim Unsworth articles in *NCR*, five books, and frequent essays in *U.S. Catholic, America, Ligourian, The Critic,* and many other publications.

That first article brought us another treasure—our friendship with Cardinal Bernardin. When he came to Chicago, I met him at an archdiocesan Environment and Art Commission meeting. He said, "I want to talk to you about Tim's article. I got it on the day they were having a going-away party for me in Cincinnati. I though it was so funny that I brought it to the party and read it to everyone." I invited him to dinner to meet Tim, and he ended up coming to our home at least once every year from then on. We remember every one of his visits, but especially those after his cancer was diagnosed. He talked a lot about praying, and admitted that when he was in pain it is very hard for him to pray. Tim knows that feeling now.

In 1987, when I was offered early retirement from Loyola University, where I was a Professor of Fine Arts, I said I would do it only if Tim would also quit his job and write full time. He did; so I did. And the years from then until Tim's hip replacement surgery in 2006 were rich and rewarding. We rose early, walked to Starbucks, had coffee, read *The New York Times,* then walked back to begin our day at our two computers. We both published extensively during those years. And we traveled—often two trips to Europe in a year. Tim loved to write. Often, while watching TV in the evening, I would see him back at his computer, adding a phrase or idea he had just thought up to an article for *NCR.*

Tim does not write anymore. He cannot walk or even sit up. This wonderful man—who was so funny, wise and fluent when television crews would interview him when they needed witty, independent, lay commentary on current Church problems or events—even has trouble speaking now. But he is still alert and aware. He is very pleased that this book of his articles from *NCR* is being published. We are thankful to Greg Pierce, Bob McClory and Tom Roberts for making it happen.

Tim loved getting e-mail responses to his *NCR* articles. We still correspond with many of his readers. If this book gives you pleasure or renews your faith in the promise of Vatican II, please send us an email at unsworth3150@comcast.net. We'd love to hear from you.

This is the first article that Tim submitted to the National Catholic Reporter. It launched his journalism career. He wrote it a month after Bernardin was named archbishop of Chicago and it ran in NCR ten days before Bernardin's official installation.

Eat at a deli, walk to work, sell the mansion

Dear Archbishop Bernardin:

The other day I was eating a Polish with everything at a Rush Street deli not far from where I work. It was crowded with a variety of people as interesting as the variety of lunch meals and cheeses inside the counter.

A man, dressed in basic clergy black with collar, came in. He took his place in line, waited his turn, and ordered a salami and Swiss to go. My wife looked up and said: "That's the Episcopal Bishop of Chicago."

One of your duties as the new archbishop of the largest diocese in America should be to go to a deli, wait in line and order a salami and Swiss to go. Pay your money and leave, and pick a bench in a nearby park. Then eat your sandwich while you watch the people. (There's a huge building going up right across from the chancery. You could join others in watching the workmen while you eat your sandwich. People would most likely walk up to you and talk with you—people who don't have an appointment.)

I pass the chancery almost every day. (Cynics and other wounded Christians often call it the Kremlin.) Anyway, I couldn't help but notice the good-looking temporary administrator of the archdiocese who ran the store following the death of John Patrick Cody. He emerged from his chauffeur-driven car and whirled through the revolving doors en route to work. I understand that he's a hard worker and that he has really cut down on some of the huge piles of paperwork that grew during the cardinal's last months.

> An archbishop on a CTA bus could convert half the bus population.

I asked about the chauffeur and was informed by someone who works inside the chancery that "it's because the archdiocese is a corporation sole and the lawyers don't want Father Keating involved in an accident that would involve the corporation" (Monsignor John Keating is temporary administrator of the archdiocese).

Oh. (But that sure cuts out going to the deli.)

Your next priority should be to take a chance. Walk to work. If you can't drive because you're a corporation sole, then walk along Lake Shore Drive. Or take the 151 bus. An archbishop on a CTA bus could convert half the bus population.

If the walk is too far, move in closer. There's a nice, gray house on Superior—I think the number is 21—which is owned by the archdiocese, just a few yards from Michigan Avenue and your office.

You could sell the old mansion on North State Parkway. It's an embarrassment. The only people who can afford to live in mansions like that are the archbishop of Chicago and Hugh Hefner. Hefner wants such symbols. You don't need them. Move to the place on Superior. (Ironically, it was once Hefner's office.) It would be best to move out of that haunted house, so spooky with clericalism, triumphalism and a host of other ghosts.

TIM UNSWORTH

These, then, are my three top priorities for you: eat a sandwich in a deli. Take a walk of a bus. Move out of that house.

After that, the rest will be easy. It won't seem too risky to remove the Telex to the Vatican from your mansion and to just write them occasional letters. It will be even easier to call your attorney, Don Reuben, and tell him that the archdiocese will make public all records pertaining to the recent investigation and that he should present them to you in an orderly fashion without delay. Indeed, you could tell him that you plan to publish a thorough report together with complete answers to all questions in a subsequent issue of the *Chicago Catholic* just as soon as they can be put in readable form.

It will take some time, but if your staff are informed that you walked to work, they might be quick to recognize that you mean it when you say: "I want a complete accounting of all church assets, including our stock portfolio, made public within the next 90 days."

Then, call your communications people and tell them to answer questions as quickly and as accurately as they can. That will be hard at the start. There are so many unanswered questions, but it has got to be done because the faithful have lost faith. They will need to see and effort to erase all those "no comments." You'll need a communications person, but try not to have such a person around when you answer questions, as if he/she were a lawyer at your side during an adversary proceeding. The pattern of communications in recent years has been all too depressing. In most instances, it was one of outright denial coupled with criticism of those who were asking. The next step was a qualified denial coupled with increased criticism of those who were asking. This was followed by a qualified admission with much of the same criticism. Finally, there would be an admission of the truth. Not very inspiring.

You have been touted as a communicator. We would welcome

that. You have already said that, "When people are informed and involved, they will give even more." I applaud that. It must happen here because, at present, this great archdiocese has lost faith in its leaders.

Your *Chicago Catholic* isn't a very good paper: secretive, selective, defensive, patronizing, paranoid. And often guilty of the very things they complain of in the secular press. At times, they've raised issues that aren't even true. When denied, the paper hardly bothers to acknowledge the denial. If they do, it's often with a cry that says: "Well, you sounded that way!" Its articles are so predictable that one has only to read the opening paragraph. It conceals far more than it reveals. It is a paper under siege, incapable of thoughtful dialogue.

Last week, it contained a quote from Monsignor Brackin, who said he hoped that the new (then unnamed) archbishop would not do anything for a year until "he found out how we do things in Chicago." Good Lord, don't do that! Come in and open the windows! Come and preach to us! Come and serve while leading. (Monsignor Francis Brackin is the vicar general of the archdiocese.)

Then, read a book. One that you like and one that speaks to your pastoral concerns. Review it in the *Chicago Catholic*, or in the public press or on TV—whatever. Use it to teach. Let all know that you have a mind; that theology is not suspect; that you are a shepherd first and a businessman second. (In fact, there shouldn't be a second. Let other's do that.)

Years ago, the church in Chicago had only an occasional need for a legal counsel. Allowing for the increase in litigation in our society, I still feel that the relationship between the client and lawyer in this archdiocese has grown much too close. The whispers of the attorney drown out the voices of those crying out for help or recognition. I'm informed that the late archbishop had a direct line to his attorney's office. Pull it out. If you don't, you could get strangled by it.

There's a guy named John Shea up at the seminary. He's a Scripture man or parable man. Something like that. But go get him and talk with him at least once a month. You do not always need a lawyer, but you shouldn't be without a theologian. And Shea is good.

The leaders of this city will invite you to dinner—to size you up and see how they can use you. You have to go, I suppose, but just as soon as you're finished with all of this, start having meals with your fellow

You do not always need a lawyer, but you shouldn't be without a theologian.

priests. Nothing formal. Just a buffet from those catering-house aluminum pans. And listen. I'm told that you're very good at that. You'll hear a lot and meet some very good men. Later, you can organize all you have heard. Don't try to do it at first or you won't hear.

There are a lot of good things happening in this archdiocese, but they are happening in spite of rather than because of the leadership. Now, there remains a huge moat between the pilgrim church and the cathedral church—so wide that one fine priest once said to me that the only help the institutional church is to him is to get a discount on a car. Privately, the priests often refer to John Patrick Cody as "Herod"—the one who killed all the babies. You have a lot of hidden anger to pull from these men before they will hear you with the ears of understanding.

There's a better than even chance that you'll get a red hat at the next consistory. That's a terrible burden to anticipate because it means that Rome will be watching you and, worse, you might be watching Rome. I hope not. I hope that you'll charge on as if Rome were not marking your paper.

Oh, about Rome. Be sure to share some of our wealth with the agencies in the Vatican who aid the poor throughout the world. But no gifts to the curia, please. No libraries for their homes. No fancy cars. No vacations in this country. No $1000 mass cards. That's bribery and thievery. Chicago Catholics are pretty well off. But they work hard for their money. It deserves a better place.

> 〰 Let your monument be some carefully wrought pastorals.

You'll be the boss of the Extension Society [headquartered here in Chicago]. Please see to it that the monies donated to this society are used for the purposes indicated. Don't use it for other purposes, even if you are the boss.

Read another book. Or write a pastoral letter. But it can be on other topics than abortion. Abortion is a terrible thing. One writer likened it to a mine disaster, with all those bodies buried inside. But speak with a softer, more understanding voice on this issue. There is something terribly frightening about many of those pro-life people who march in the St. Patrick's Day parade carrying white wooden rifles as a symbol of their fight. Holler at the shame of abortion if you must, but do so at the door of your mansion that you are holding open for the unwanted children or the pregnant mothers.

Back to your pastoral. Bishops should write good ones, or get people who can do so. Years ago, when this was a building church, bishops went around town with models of churches in the trunks of their cars. Building isn't in anymore. So, let your monument be some carefully wrought pastorals.

Take a lunch break and go back to the deli. By this time, people will be talking to you more and telling you things. Talk with the cop on the corner. Cops have great, human stories to tell. They exaggerate them a lot, but add salt and they'll come out about right.

Take a ride on the subway or el. Look at the people. Look hard. It will do a lot for your pastoral letters. It will help you remember and focus after you get back from the White House. You must bring the institutional church closer to the people.

Go and say a prayer at Walter Imbiorski's grave. He was a priest in this archdiocese who did some very fine things both here in Chicago and nationwide. Cana and pre-Cana. Christian Family Movement. Some years ago, he resigned from the priesthood and married, without church approval. When he died suddenly, the church refused him a church burial. Go and pray and heal that wound that is so symbolic of other such wounds inflicted in the name of discipline.

Then open your home to other resigned priests. Bring them in and listen to them and ask how you can use them. Many would rush to be of service. Some would return to active service. All remain your brother priests.

Listen to nuns. Some of those outfits of nuns are solving their problems in a more creative way than the men of the church.

Support ERA. Else, if anything, the anti-ERA people will not give you their cold, heartless and paranoid embrace.

Pick five good auxiliaries for starters. Pastoral men. Try for a good mix. Pick one Roman. Maybe Keating. You'll need someone to say grace at political dinners. Keating has worked hard and he's good-looking. In time, he'll get a diocese of his own, and men like him have been known to get religion once they have a place of their own. But make the remaining four pastoral types. Maybe a black guy. More likely, a Latino. Ideally, however, get good guys without too much regard to skin or blood.

Then use them—not simply for work you don't want to do. Use them as decision-makers as well as healers. Give up some of your enormous power to them. You'll still have plenty left.

The auxiliaries should be local people. They had some real good ones here over the years. Guys with energy, ideas—and a lot of devotion. Sound out your priests on who they want. You might find that they make very good picks. Trust them. Think as a priest and look through priest's eyes at your fellow priests.

Don't let the politicians use you. If you could hear how they speak of you and other bishops, you would blush and be angry. Don't get too close. It will make it much harder for you to remind them of their obligations.

> ～ Don't get too close to politicians. It will make it much harder for you to remind them of their obligations.

Don't go to parades unless they are religious ones. Don't go to the St. Patrick's Day parade and then stay away from the peace march. Don't march with Poles and then not march with blacks. Every parade in this town is a political one. Parades say too much about choices. You'll get tainted.

A good friend of mine suggested that you look up Monsignor Dan Cantwell. He was a prominent and much-loved priest here in town. Today, he is somewhere in West Virginia, working with retarded adults. No matter how deeply you cut into Dan, you'll still find a priest. Bring him home and make him your confessor.

Maybe you could lure Monsignor Jack Egan back. He's gotten rather involved at Notre Dame. He might not be comfortable back here anymore. But his return could signal that new ideas are allowed once more. (Monsignor Jack Egan is assistant to the president of the University of Notre Dame.)

I know a guy who could make you a plain, simple, non-kissing ring.

And instead of spending a lot of time designing your crest and picking a motto, why not drop the whole thing? Have a motto if you like. But make it fit. *Servum Servorum Dei* (servant of the servants of God) doesn't fit too well on the back of a limo.

Oh, and those pictures—those terrible heavy oils—that so soon follow on the heels of an installation. They run about $100 each and there's heavy pressure to hang them all over town in every church, school, hall or whatnot. That's cult. Ask the institutions to just send you the $100 and give the money to the poor.

Some awfully good laity around Chicago. I don't know how you can listen to them all. But our concerns could be reduced to no more than 100, and 25 of these are the most pressing. Do some networking with us. Then respond.

You'll have time. You've got a job where you can't be fired. That puts you in the top one per cent of all people. You'll be in office until you're 75. This will be your last job, so there's no need to spend much time on your ambitions. Settle down. Sure, you could become the bishop-maker in America, like Francis Spellman of New York years ago. Hell, you could run for pope. But neither of these is a smart option.

The papers have hawked your resume. Your picture is on every street corner, peering from those newspaper-dispensing machines. You show great promise. A few friends of mine at the chancery appear very pleased. At my parish, after mass on Sunday, there were enough good words spoken about you to do a eulogy. You could bring us the energy and pride in our faith of a Mundelein, the kindness of a Stritch and the fine mind of a Meyer (previous Chicago archbishops, Cardinals George Mundelein, Samuel Stritch, Albert Meyer).

That is it for you, bishop. Enjoy it. You'll get lots of strokes—everything from children waving to *Ecce Sacerdos Magnus* (or whatever that narcissistic tune is called). You'll get a red hat. You get to park anywhere. And you never have to wait on line. You'll get lots of travel and, after death in a private room, you'll get a helluva funeral.

That's enough for one man.

In fact, it's enough to send you to a Rush Street deli for a hot dog, just so you won't forget your Ash Wednesday *"memento, homo, quia pulvis es..."* ("remember, man, that you are dust").

Upstairs or down, it's one church—January 20, 1984

Here Tim took a look at two liturgy styles in his parish church. He's not preferring one over the other, just helping himself and his readers get adjusted to the world of change.

Upstairs, downstairs, you pick your pious practice

I worship in a split-level parish. The upstairs-downstairs arrangement permits a liturgical schizophrenia that is peculiarly satisfying to most parishioners.

Upstairs, mashed-potato-and-gravy Catholics worship under a Byzantine dome before a chorus line of aged statues, including two angels with electric light torches who look dangerously like altar girls.

Downstairs, yogurt-and-tofu-Christians clap their hands before a table altar with a billboard-size background that is generally a rainbow of meaningful messages.

Upstairs, polyester-and-wool people sing to the dignified sounds of a choir and organ. Downstairs, designer-jeans-and-jogging-shoes people sing to guitar, tambourine and piano.

Upstairs, the faithful are shaped like Pillsbury doughboys. Downstairs, it's borderline anorexia. Upstairs, it's dentures and communion in the mouth. Downstairs, it's fluorides and communion under both species.

I divide my time between both churches. Upstairs confirms my past; downstairs makes me stretch my ego boundaries to meet the future.

The music downstairs has great energy, even if the guitar player seems to be doing double-dutch and the tunes sound like variations on "Found a Peanut." The upstairs music is a familiar peg on the wall of the soul on which one can hang a ragged voice.

Downstairs is SRO every Sunday—a tribute to the rhythm method practiced by the faithful upstairs.

Upstairs is not pre-Tridentine. Far from it. The long-haired acolytes have ribbons in their hair, and families tend to do more upstairs praying to—than downstairs interfacing with—the Almighty.

The word of God is the same in both places, and the priests move up and down on alternate Sundays with the ease of switching from AM to FM. The homilies sound only a little different—most likely because an involved congregation will affect a speaker about as much as he affects them.

Upstairs is Faith and Abraham and Peter. Downstairs is Hope, Isaac and John the Evangelist.

Upstairs is a mine of wisdom; downstairs is a university of talent.

Both congregations meet during social functions and in support groups. The broken glass of failed marriages and the disease of alcoholism seem to be about equally divided between both levels. Both churches meet in support groups at the parish center. The parish is a supermarket of more than 40 groups—all offering some kind of spiritual, intellectual or social vitamin or antibiotic.

Upstairs may wince a bit over bulletin announcements that there is a seminar on sex and the single person—or a discussion on how the gays in the community contribute to the life of the parish. But their anxiety may be reduced by the food for the poor left in the vestibule of the upstairs church by the downstairs faithful, or the gift of the

Eucharist brought to their hospital beds by the young singles.

Going downstairs is therapeutic for me. It forces me to test the strength of the intellectual convictions reached long before the emotional roots are touched.

The majority of the downstairs worshipers have never been to benediction. They don't have to erase the "Tantum Ergo" in order to sing "Jesus Is My Main Squeeze," or whatever the current hit is. They are relaxed, confident and a little impatient with the traditional norms and customs they had little to do with shaping. Vatican II is history to them. Their church has a more secular than sacred foundation, and they can readily keep pace with rapid change. Their faith issues are tied to social problems rather than problems involved with worship and canon law.

> Going downstairs is therapeutic for me. It forces me to test the strength of the intellectual convictions reached long before the emotional roots are touched.

They chat casually before the liturgy begins, laugh easily at the pulpit humor, embrace generously at the kiss of peace and organize instant brunches after mass.

Not long ago, I was edging down the crowded center aisle downstairs, approaching the nonexistent altar rail for communion.

For a middle-aged Charlie Brown, it's a time of high anxiety. White or whole wheat? With or without wine? In the mouth or in the hand? Should I go to the bearded pastor or muscle into the line where a terminal preppie is dispensing the Eucharist with sculptured fingers?

I decide to split my vote. Bread from the priest. Wine from the pretty preppie.

The choir was warming up its amplifiers for the communion hymn when I spotted a 10-year-old girl half kneeling and half hanging out of the pew.

She could have used a handkerchief. Her long hair had a thousand parts and she most likely had a reversible-raincoat name, such as Tiffany Sanchez.

She sang with unfiltered, unbuttoned abandon. This little girl was growing into a faith that had no mixed messages for her. With all those unborn children inside her she will carry the church into the next century.

> No matter how poorly we perceive the future church, we could hardly find a better place to entrust our faith than in the pure voice of that runny-nosed kid.

No matter how poorly we perceive the future church, we could hardly find a better place to entrust our faith than in the pure voice of that runny-nosed kid. They can revise canon law to their heart's content, but she gets to pass on the tradition.

Who knows? Maybe she'll be a priest. Most likely, there'll be an upstairs church in her life just as there will be a downstairs church for her children.

When I was a kid, my pastor came to the classroom and shoved slides of Lourdes upside down into a wheezy projector. He was a Lourdes groupie. (Finally, the parish ran some rigged bingo games to buy him a ticket to Lourdes, where he promptly got sick.)

Today, my pastor jogs and often reads poetry from the pulpit. But both preached the same gospel and creed; both kept love alive, and both pass on the faith tradition.

Richard P. McBrien has written that we need not be threatened by modernization. "It is a process," he said, "which confirms rather than undermines the church's historical message: that we are all brothers and sisters under God in Christ and that we must love one another and work unceasingly for the unity of the world."

Some years ago, Karl Rahner received an honorary degree from John Carroll University in Cleveland. In accepting the award, he cited God's message to Elijah in the Old Testament.

"Arise," the messenger said, "a long journey lies ahead of you."

The church is a borderless country. My friend Robert says that you can't reach the stars unless you reach all the rivers inside your heart. That little girl will carry the church on those journeys up those rivers long after we are buried under regulation-size stone in a regulation-size plot in one of those Catholic cemeteries.

As long as the church encourages us to reach for the stars while exploring the rivers, the good dirt of which we are made should continue to produce the flowers of Christianity that we all dream of sharing with one another.

Conservatives fear change, lack 'nose for future'
—March 2, 1984

In this column Tim openly acknowledges his liberal leanings and takes a few whacks at both liberal and conservative "politically correct" thinking. In typical fashion he does so with plenty of humor and not a hint of mean spiritedness.

Knee-jerk is still a jerk, no matter what your politics

The introduction of altar girls—knee-jerk liberals euphemistically call them mass servers—may mean the end of Christian civilization as we know it.

At least that's the way some conservatives would have us think.

A conservative, according to one dictionary, is one who tends to favor the existing order and to regard proposals for change with distrust.

Well, I'm for that. I come completely unglued when someone messes up my desktop. At the office, when an interoffice memo announces the introduction of another computer software package, I start whining and sniveling.

I treasure existing order. Perhaps I'm a closet conservative.

Having worked at three large universities, I've had ample opportunity to observe liberals and conservatives. I've developed a raised-eyebrow distrust of many university liberals. My soft research has shown that many intellectual liberals are functional conservatives.

Further, the more liberal an institution's reputation, the more conservative it tends to function internally.

Years ago, as a teacher in Catholic high schools, I noted that the most liberal priests were often the meanest in the confessional. It was as if they were personally offended by the same old dirty wash that teenagers brought in to be cleaned.

> I treasure existing order. Maybe I'm a closet conservative.

"Man," the students used to say, "there was everything in there but the rubber hose."

The students preferred the gray-haired priest they called Colonel Sanders, who listened patiently to the tales of their fall from grace and then urged them to try harder and gave them penances that fit the crimes.

There are times when I feel positively schizophrenic myself.

I'm opposed to abortion, for example, but strident pro-lifers leave me cold.

I'm against capital punishment, but I get furious at the sight of blessed-out people standing outside a prison gate, shedding tears about a guy who has reduced some family to chopped liver.

The conservative side of me applauds President Reagan's efforts to appoint an official ambassador to the Vatican. The liberal side of me quivers at the prospects of the type of person he would appoint. The Vatican is a great listening place, but an ambassador who is a Knight of Everything, a World War III enthusiast and a friend of the curia could be a funnel for even more conservative gossip about the American Church.

I've rarely met a bishop I didn't like—even the very few who couldn't think much deeper than a Sears, Roebuck and Co. floor-walker. Most are good, solid oak—warm, compassionate men who actually pray when they are alone—in spite of the fact that they are largely conservative.

≋ My quarrel may not be with conservatives, but rather with reactionaries—people who view any change in the church as some kind of ecclesiastical fluoride.

On the other hand, I've met some fascinating liberal theologians—individuals with the clarity and depth of expression of a $5,000 stereo system and the feeling mechanism of a retarded lobster.

I'm more often accused of being liberal than conservative. The sock-it-to-them letters I get from liberals generally address what I've said but suggest that I didn't go far enough. Although rarely accusing me of being a deep thinker, the letters from liberals do not engage in the *ad hominum* attacks of the conservative writers. The latter proclaim that I'm immature and adolescent—barbs that make me want to throw my yo-yo at the nearest member of Opus Dei.

A conservative priest once called my mother-in-law and whispered, "Tell Tim to back off." I've been looking over my shoulder ever since, terrified that I'll be found at the bottom of an abandoned baptismal font wrapped in back issues of *L'Osservatore Romano*.

Yet, one five-star archbishop told me that he enjoyed what I wrote. He added that he had brought one piece to a party and read it as part of the entertainment. It was a compliment that left me a bit frazzled.

Conservatives always seem to know how much spiritual mileage they're getting. Liberals don't even know the difference between the "seven gifts" and the "twelve fruits."

Perhaps, this is all simply verbal ping-pong. My quarrel may not be with conservatives, but rather with reactionaries—people who view any change in the church as some kind of ecclesiastical fluoride.

Tom Fox, who edits this treacherous birdcage liner, has described being conservative as "knowing our center and the spot from which we will not leave and from which we can look forward with great confidence."

The wonderfully playful artist Joan Miro once said that it's essential to have your feet firmly planted in order to jump in the air.

Conservative reactionaries canonize the past but have no nose for the future. It seems to me that their fear of the future is actually a hatred of the present. They appear to be profoundly unhappy people who find the most unusual fences to hide behind. Reactionaries spend a great deal of time making motes into beams. Liberals may drown one in new ideas, but reactionaries seldom offer any new ideas. They prefer to investigate those who do.

My friend Robert once studied to be rabbi. Now, he is a rare and wonderful full-time poet who views religious institutions as seashores.

"Their very foundation is the sand," he said, "full of wisdom. The ocean writes books there. There is lots of driftwood and sometimes sharks or the rumors of sharks. But there are beautiful shells, some so delicate, so perfect, so full of glory."

Helen Keller used to say that security is mostly a superstition. It seems, however, that lay conservatives prefer the security of an unchanging theology and discipline and that clerical conservatives equate any change with the loss of authority.

I'm concerned. I wish everyone could be a wishy-washy Charlie Brown Christian like myself.

Those Roman soldiers knew enough to shoot craps ever the seamless garment at the foot of the cross so that they wouldn't ruin it.

I hope we don't tear the robe apart with our antics.

The "old man" in this story was Frank J. Morman, Tim's father-in-law. The "old woman" was Marie Morman, Frank's wife of over 60 years. The priest was Fr. Len Dubi from their parish church. Frank was like a traveler, Tim later observed, "sitting on the couch with his bags packed, impatient to leave."

A guided tour of Gethsemane

The old man was curled up in fetal position on the bed. His once sinewy frame was now hung with spotted, sagging skin. Only his bald head was smooth. The eyes were cataract-blurred; the ears heard only high pitched voices and his teeth had long since departed this world.

"What's wrong with him," said an earlier nurse, "is that everything he's got is 84 years old." The nurse attending him now whispered, "It won't be long. There's death in this room. You learn to sense it."

The tall, bearded priest was kneeling by the bed. His long frame bent easily over the old man's soup-bone body.

It was as if he were talking on an old wall telephone. The tall priest prayed the "Our Father" into the old man's ear. He followed with a "Hail Mary" and then turned the old man gently on his back before opening his pyx, which contained the body of Christ.

The old man couldn't take the eucharist. The priest touched the host to the old man's lips and gently passed it to his wife of more than 61 years. Then the tall priest put his long-fingered hand on the old man's bald head and prayed some more.

He closed the prayer with "I love you, Frank." It was a scene with more emotion than a four-star liturgy in the Sistine Chapel.

It was a moment when we discover that what we would like to be true is true.

> Too often, clergy and laity would rather be organizing some meaningful endeavor that spares all of us the blushing intimacy of being Mary rather than Martha.

It seems to me that God can easily become a conglomerate in our faith perception. Even the paradoxical metaphor of the trinity seems to enhance the notion of God as a corporate logo.

Surely, for too many of us, God has taken on a corporate identity that exists independently of what individual men and women actually experience for themselves. At times, we get so involved with group activity, addictive liturgies and a bewildering variety of political and social issues that the essential one-on-one relationship with God can become an embarrassing interruption.

Too often, clergy and laity would rather be organizing some meaningful endeavor that spares all of us the blushing intimacy of being Mary rather than Martha.

There are times when we would rather organize a support group for kids who didn't get Cabbage Patch dolls for Christmas than to pray to an ear of a dying man.

Weeks before, the old man had said to an older priest, "God just forgot one thing when he made us, Father. He should of put a switch right here so you could just turn off when you are ready to go."

The old man did have more reason for dying than he did for living. But the tall priest just told him "Frank, relax. Jesus isn't ready for you yet. He'll take you when he's ready. You've got to learn to just relax in his arms the way a baby does in the arms of his mother."

That's our problem. We are terrified to give up the illusion that we are in control. We are more comfortable living from the neck up—doing good—rather than contemplating God.

Zen theologians tell us that our spiritual development lies in recognizing that we do not breathe—we are breathed. But, probably because of our fear of letting go, we come to experience only faint glimmers of such transcendence.

The glimmers are simply hints of what our parish discussion groups tell us is to come but at least they spare us the blindness of total darkness.

In the weeks that followed, the old man tried to communicate as much as his weakened condition and occasionally wandering mind would permit. He was searching for an effective language in which he could talk to God—some words that would get him across the border of where human nature ended and true religious experience began.

It wasn't easy. It's always easier for us to go to some meaningful prayer service and hold hands—like a huge jumper cable—and pray for something as lofty as peace or rapid weight loss. It's much harder when we must pray to an absent God.

The old man finally settled on "Thy will be done." When the priest prayed with him after that, the old man would pause at those four words from the familiar *Pater Noster* and virtually shout, "Thy will be done!"—as if to use these words as a battering ram through the wall of sickness, sadness and depression within himself to the true God-feeling he was seeking.

Watching the tall priest working one-on-one with the old man was a guided tour of Gethsemane. It was an affirmation of priesthood that dwarfs any other aspects of priestly ministry. However worthwhile and productive, the priest at the center of a cause—peace, justice, equality, whatever—does not approach the effectiveness of a priest leading an old man through a second birth.

Slowly, the tall priest drew the old man beyond himself—to become something other than what he was. The process took place not in some domed church or in some crowded forum, but in a small, square bedroom not much bigger than a sepulcher.

Priests are like artists. They can get caught up in their own early successes and get seduced by the applause of smiles that illuminate their processions down the center aisle. Or they can plunge back into their art for new resources to share with their people.

The tall priest—once a community activist who energized thousands—was now working soul by soul, even as he made his own journey back from alcoholism.

Gradually, the tightly wrapped old man relaxed as babies do. Dressed in his yellow golf sweater and warmed by his favorite red blanket to which he had become almost childishly attached, the old man now seemed impatient to let go. One got the feeling he was now running toward heaven—not struggling to cling to this earth.

Life, particularly an involved Christian life, can get pretty boggling. *NCR* is a weekly compendium of instant replays of numerous happenings under church steeples and in the world outside.

It can get pretty complicated. One can parse the new canon law or try to understand Bernard Lonergan's theology. (My own favorite pastime is church politics.) Or you can experience some vicarious apostolate by silk-screening Christian messages on lunch bags, "to get God back into schools," said the ad I spotted recently.

But in the end, if you're as lucky as the old man, it will get down to God, priest and pilgrim.

The old man found one final drop of blood with life in it. He used it to touch his wife's head and to kiss her almost as vigorously as he did on her porch when he met her in 1919. Then he died, like a kid falling asleep in his mother's arms.

> In the end, if you're as lucky as the old man, it will get down to God, priest and pilgrim.

Theologian Karl Barth has written a library of books that attempt to unravel the mystery of God and the sunburst of other theological conclusions that emanate from the God-feeling in all of us.

When asked to extract the most significant thought from the mountain of words such consideration produce, Barth answered, "Jesus loves me, this I know, because the Bible tells me so."

It gets pretty simple when we're running on fumes.

As soon as the old man had been carried from his small, brick home, his widow called the tall priest.

He was at a parish meeting—something to do with teenagers. But as soon as he got the message, he called the old woman and prayed with her over the phone.

After fifteen months of nursing her husband, she had already learned that suffering and joy are often hard to tell apart.

Now, all the tall priest had to do was to work one-on-one with *her*—to teach *her* to wait properly.

Bishop's letter on war and peace: prescription for pastoral leadership—May 1, 1984

The U.S. Catholic bishops approved their much discussed pastoral letter on war and peace on May 3, 1983. Tim saw the event a year later as a kind of watershed, challenging lay Catholics to become activists for justice, and he hoped the letter would be followed by similar challenges to take responsibility.

Peace I give to you

The bishops' pastoral letter on war and peace may be the biggest shot to the American church since Notre Dame invented the forward pass.

The 45,000-word document is a kind of intellectual national shrine that continues to draw pilgrims each day since the 247 bishops assembled in a Chicago hotel and voted 238-9 to approve the final text.

After 40 earlier meetings—at which, I was told, tuna salad was served every time—the bishops declared, in effect, that our best thinking is not necessarily what we've always thought and that no one should go around threatening to do what one cannot morally do.

But that's not the point of this verbal brioche. My point is that *The Challenge of Peace* may have done wonders toward curing bishops of the 97-pound-weakling syndrome that seems to have affected them of late.

Not long ago, I went to the University of Chicago to attend a symposium on the pastoral letter sponsored by the Institute for the Advanced Study of Religion of the university's divinity school.

The University of Chicago is a 180-acre brain in Chicago's Hyde

Park. It is surrounded by neighborhoods that look as if they were practice sites for the bomb. But the campus is a gothic wonderland.

The seminar was in Swift Hall—a marvelous collegiate gothic building with gargoyles, griffins, beamed ceilings, carved angels and very funny graffiti in the washroom.

Almost 40 years ago, only 300 yards from the gargoyles, some very bright humans split the atom. They did it because they heard that the Germans were going to do it. Instead, Germans surrendered. The profs kept working until nuclear energy was born. A few weeks later, two cities were blown away.

That was a time when the church was a bouillabaisse of myths, rituals, spiritually induced terror and a God who could reconcile opposites. Even at the University of Chicago, always a world-class divinity school surrounded by orbiting affiliated theology schools, very few suggested that the new sword should be delivered to the art department and made into a plowshare.

≈≈ Bishops built churches and schools and, theologically speaking, confined themselves to installing speed bumps on the pathway to heaven that made it harder to be a Catholic in fact than it did in principle.

Besides, it seems to me that 1945-era bishops weren't very excited about a public theology. They pretty much preached to their "own kind," as my mother called us. Bishops built churches and schools and, theologically speaking, confined themselves to installing speed bumps on the pathway to heaven that made it harder to be a Catholic in fact than it did in principle.

I memorized those neat little sentences about just war—phrases that spoke of a good old conventional war in which no one broke rules. Lots of St. Thomas and St. Augustine. The Trinity was God, pope and church. And, after grammar school religion, Jesus was pretty much a theological dropout.

Anyway, nearly four decades after nuclear fission, about 300 sets of tweeds and elbow patches gathered a few blocks from the Henry Moore sculpture that now marks the spot of the first atomic pile.

It was an experience to be in a room with all those earnest people—most of whom had read all 339 paragraphs of the letter. It would have made you proud to hear those scholars, who had virtually CAT-scanned the document, declaring it "a model for emulation," "a document free of creeping infallibility," "a truly ecclesial document" and a host of other plaudits.

After the three-hour session, there was a sherry and wimp food reception, a chicken dinner and a brief walk to the Rockefeller Chapel to hear Cardinal Joseph Bernardin talk about the letter.

The Cardinal, like most of his fellow bishops, is a 1950s priest. They were trained on Augustine and Aquinas and weaned on Vatican II. The best of them are men who seriously considered quitting at one time or another in the 30 or more years since most of them have been ordained.

Bernardin is the consummate 1950s priest—a man with extraordinary sonar and radar senses and a unique ability to tie his 1950s seminary training to 1980s realities.

He climbed into the high pulpit in the cathedral-size chapel and

Bernardine sought the scholars' help in formulating a theology to match the pathology of a war that will have no winners. Clerical triumphalism died on the spot.

read a prepared text that invited even more dialogue on all the issues than the white light of a potentially exploding bomb could illuminate.

Far from being dogmatic or pedantic, Bernardin seemed to say that bishops often work among their betters. He sought the scholars' help in formulating a theology to match the pathology of a war that will have no winners. Clerical triumphalism died on the spot.

What a change! One of Bernardin's ecclesiastical ancestors would not permit a Newman Club at the university, because he saw the place as a threat to the faithful. As a consequence, university professors often stropped their razor-like minds on the watered-silk cinctures of the tightly wrapped bishops.

Now, the bishops are taking another tack. The carefully crafted document is not just a new perspective on an old problem, it is a prescription for pastoral leadership.

I look for bishops to do a lot more writing in the future. They'll cover every issue from the correct amount of beeswax in church candles to statements that may cause confrontations with the White House. Their writings will bring them closer to other old-line churches but away from the newer, fundamentalist sects.

There will be local as well as national letters on liturgy, economy, social issues and inspirational messages. The Christian development of the people of the church will be given a higher priority than the development of buildings.

Most people welcome periodic insistencies on some sort of standard. The bishops have now had the excitement of challenging us. In doing so, they have been challenged themselves.

The Challenge of Peace will cause American bishops to adjust their mission. Its publication is an occasion of growth for us all.

I was crossing Michigan Avenue on May 3, 1983, the day the

bishops voted on the final text. It was a bit late, and a few quartets of bishops were walking north on Michigan, probably in search of a restaurant.

I had heard on the office radio that the document had been approved. The bishops seemed to be walking taller.

I wanted to shout: "God bless your indelible marks!" But then, he already had.

Tim was an avid fan of Flannery O'Connor. He like her determined Catholicism, her sense of the mystery behind all visible things and her insight into the messiness involved in the meeting of God and humanity.

A novelist without fear of imagination or religion

This is the 20th anniversary of her death. (She died in August 1964, at 39, a victim of lupus.) She left a literary estate of four novels, a book of short stories, a collection of ten essays and a generous volume of letters to a chorus of people to whom she wrote from 1948 until 1964.

She has withstood the test of time. After more than 20 years, her thoughts are still on sale in bookstores; her novels are read in any good modern English class, and most anthologies contain at least one of her short stories. You can—and should—buy the entire collection in paperback for about $35.

Flannery O'Connor's death was a mine disaster: she died with all those unmined words inside her. But she left enough to guarantee her a place in American and modern Christian thought.

You could beneficially stop reading this essay now and rush to her sentences. You'd be way ahead.

What Flannery O'Connor had was an eye—the organ she said "eventually involves the whole personality and as much of the world as can be got into it."

It was an intensely Catholic eye—one so obvious that there were those who said she could not be an artist because she was a R.C. To which she replied, "Because I am a Catholic, I cannot afford to be less than an artist."

She was, she said, a Catholic who believed in "the God of Abraham, Isaac and Jacob and not of the philosophers and scholars."

Sally Fitzgerald wrote of her that her faith was "her intellectual and spiritual taproot, and it deepened and spread outward in her with the years."

O'Connor could have drawn sneers from the intellectual community for her adherence to the church. But those who would sneer would risk one of her steely glances. She had her reservations about the church, but believed that it was her church to have reservations about and that the membership benefits far out-weighed the demands that the church made on her.

If her eye spotted pious trash in so-called Catholic novels, she never hesitated to call it pious trash—no matter how important the author. She once suggested the late Cardinal Francis Spellman's treacly novel, *The Foundling*, could best be used as a doorstop.

"When the Catholic novelist closes his own eyes and tries to see with the eyes of the church," she said, "the result is another addition to that large body of pious trash for which we have so long been famous."

While guarding her "eye," O'Connor accepted Christian dogma pretty much as it was handed to her because she thought it was the only thing in the world that guarded and respected mystery.

But she treated her religion as most homesteaders of old treated their property—she guarded what had been passed on to her, but she did what she wished with it.

"The church," she wrote, "should make the novelist a better novelist." Any limitations designed to make straight the way should never "make tight the straitjacket." For her, any impoverishment of the imagination meant an impoverishment of one's religious life as well.

Good and evil in life as well as literature were, for O'Connor, not simply a problem to be solved but a mystery to be endured.

O'Connor's eye—like our own faith search—was not focused on things meant to please everybody or even a special few. Rather, she wrote—and lived—for the good of what she was writing or doing.

The Catholic press—especially the diocesan press—frequently chided her for her novels, which, among other things, lacked the neat, clean and happy endings that rewarded good and punished evil.

"You write what you can," she answered. "And you become what you can."

For O'Connor, a belief in a fixed dogma could not fix what goes on in life or blind a believer to it. A person "wanders about in life," she wrote, "caught in a maze of guilt he can't identify, trying to reach a God he can't approach, a God powerless to approach him."

> For O'Connor, any impoverishment of the imagination meant an impoverishment of one's religious life as well.

Being a Christian reminded her of marriage. "When you get into it," she said during a lecture, "you find it is the beginning, not the end, of the struggle to make love work."

Yet, those who were troubled by her failure to tidy up the perverseness of human nature that she saw around her were often less tolerant of that same handicapped nature than she was. The lesson here may be that one can tidy up best by accepting the mess.

Faith is not a pacemaker that a well-meaning priest implants in a Christian soul. For O'Connor, all human nature vigorously resisted grace because grace changed us and change was painful.

"Human nature is so faulty," she said, "that it can resist any amount of grace and most of the time it does. The church does well to hold its own. You are asking that she show a profit."

She had a center from which she would not budge, a confidence that said where there is no belief there is no drama and a sense that our best feelings stem from the realization we cannot walk on water and are not required to do so in order to be Christians.

> For O'Connor, all human nature vigorously resisted grace because grace changed us and change was painful.

From Pierre Teilhard de Chardin she learned about "passive diminishment"—a phrase having something to do with accepting what cannot be changed. Such acceptance seemed to bring out what was genuine in her.

Read her again. She might cause each of us to rearrange the furniture in our own soul, to shed about 50 pounds of libido, to tame an insatiable want gland and to rise from the ashes of our own compulsive little egos.

This column drew a large response from readers—perhaps because many parishes have someone like Jim who is a permanent fixture. And maybe it moved readers to show the sensitivity to their outcasts that Tim's parish showed to Jim.

The back-row preacher

There is a man living in the back pew of our parish church. He has been there since late fall 1984, when the cold weather drove him in from the kiosk in the park.

Jim is your basic homeless man. He looks rounder than he probably is because his body serves as his coatrack. His pew holds about four plastic bags of belongings, most of which seem to be old newspapers.

Jim reads a lot. He often sits on the bus bench on Clark Street, reading a discarded *Chicago Tribune*. So he's got to know that the country is booming. He just ought to pull himself up by his plastic bag handles and get to work.

Benedict Joseph Labre was born near Boulogne in 1748, the eldest of fifteen children of a prosperous shopkeeper. Between 1766 and 1770, he made several attempts to join one or another religious order. But he kept getting rejected because he was too young or too delicate. Largely, however, he was rejected because the people in charge thought Benedict didn't have both oars in the water.

The sisters who taught me at St. Alice's were big on Benedict Joseph Labre. Perhaps it was because the Depression was still on and there were poor people everywhere.

I wasn't poor. My father was superintendent of a bakery. The bakeries kept going during the Depression. Breadlines were the one constant image of the Depression. We had a warm house with an electric button upstairs that let you turn on the gas under the hot-water tank in the basement. And we had a 1932 Dodge with mohair seats. But there were families with fathers out of work and the nuns were often after me to ask my father to find a job for someone at the bakery.

For the sisters, Benedict was a model that at least offered some pie in the sky when there wasn't much pie around.

Benedict Joseph Labre died 203 years ago. But I may know more about him than I do about my fellow parishioner Jim.

Jim just came in one cold day and settled in. No forms to complete to determine whether he qualified. It's entirely possible that in one of his plastic bags is a bundle of passbooks bound with a rubber band that show balances in six figures.

The parish must have a staff of ten, including a certified, vaccinated social worker. You would have thought that one of them could have devised a form that would certify his bottom-rung status in the social order. I asked Ann, the caseworker, and, with the breezy indifference of a committed Christian, she said, "I don't know anything about him, Tim. He's just there."

Once Benedict Joseph Labre overcame the handicap of being considered someone whose porch light wasn't always on, he was declared a saint and card-cataloged as a mendicant.

Mendicant is nice word for beggar. Today, our no-nonsense administration calls a bum a bum and is dedicated to weeding out anyone who is trying to swipe money from those loyal defense contractors and their designer toilet seats.

Jim could be called a mendicant. The zippered hood on his outer coat becomes a cowl when he ventures out. But maybe—just maybe—like Benedict, Jim is a contemporary Western example of an as-

TIM UNSWORTH

cetical vocation better known in the East. Maybe Jim is a pilgrim or a wandering holy man. Maybe, if one could come to know Jim better, one could find points of resemblance with the Greek *saloi* or the Russian *yurodivy*—"fools for Christ's sake."

The brothers who taught me in high school used to feed the hungry at their novitiate door. "You've got to feed them," one old brother used to say. "You never know which one them might be Him."

Jim doesn't get around that much. He may be older than Benedict. He is rarely a mile from the church. His schedule seems to be tied to one of the city's "Meals on Wheels" vehicles, which provide a diet that is balanced with dumpster pickings.

> "You've got to feed them," one old brother used to say. "You never know which one them might be Him."

Jim attends every mass on Sundays and weekdays. That's a lot of liturgy for a man who may not be a registered Catholic parishioner. The liturgies at St. Clement's are awfully good and the homilists seem to compete with one another for good preaching. They hold forth from an attractive Byzantine pulpit, to which some earlier pastor seems to have mistakenly affixed a white angel doing a reverse stuff shot with the earth.

Jim preaches from the back row.

George L. Mosse, whom I've never heard of, has written that "mendicants encouraged emotional religion." Maybe that is what Jim does for St. Clement's. His back-row homilies are so filled with silence that they force thought and action in the rest of us.

Following the final blessing, people often try to press money on Jim. He always refuses. Sometimes people's need to give outdistances others' need to receive.

Benedict Joseph Labre settled down in Rome in 1774, spending his days in the churches and his nights on the Colosseum. In time, his health failed and he had to enter a home for the destitute. In 1783, he collapsed in church and was carried to the back room of a butcher shop, where he died. He was 35.

In a way, Benedict Joseph Labre was lucky. He was canonized in 1881. At least he got some belated recognition. Today, an estimated 50,000 mendicants are in New York alone. Today, in a country that boasts one million millionaires, the rate of TB among the homeless is a hundred times that of those with homes. The homeless are six times sicker and have fourteen times more skin diseases. The homeless have diseases that are supposed to be extinct. When they die, they depart this earth in solitude—as unnoticed as a cigarette butt.

Two young men at St. Clement's are the community's sacristans. Saturday evenings, they turn on the sanctuary lights and prepare the altar for the Sunday liturgies. With the rest of the church in darkness, it's easy to forget Jim. The sacristans sometimes sing hymns as they work, because everyone likes to sing in an empty church. One night, when they reached a pause in the song, they heard a deep, resonant voice coming from the rear of the church. Jim was joining them in a song to God. From deep inside his quiet, he found a seldom-used voice.

Dolores the nun, an associate pastor without portfolio, has long wanted to provide a place to sleep for the homeless who live in the cracks of this affluent, lakefront neighborhood. Jim's presence acted as a catalyst. Now, upward of a dozen homeless men and women come to the lower church each evening, get some coffee and rolls and sleep on one of the futon-like mats around the edges of the pews. It isn't much, but it's the Ritz for those who sleep in alleys and who must worry that the bitter weather will freeze their hearts harder than a White House aide's.

Jim doesn't mix with the others. He sleeps sitting in a pew or sits along the wall, refusing one of the plastic-covered pallets.

Sally, one of the volunteers, got through Jim's quiet one night and he talked a little. He didn't make a lot of sense. His sentences weren't quite tied together. Perhaps Jim's elevator doesn't go all the way to the top. But his gentle manner, penetrating eyes and powerful presence help us keep our own balance needles from becoming skewed. Maybe Jim is as sane as St. Benedict Joseph Labre.

It's warmer now and Jim isn't always in his pew when the church lights are turned off at night. He sleeps in the park, surrounded by his shopping bags, protected by St. Benedict Joseph Labre.

≫ Jim reminds us that our dream of private success and our canonization of rugged individualism eventually so fragments us that out individualism breaks down along with our dignity.

Jim reminds us of the poverty of affluence. He reminds us that our dream of private success and our canonization of rugged individualism eventually so fragments us that out individualism breaks down along with our dignity.

Edwin Markam has a poem called "The Third Wonder." It's short. Here's the whole thing.

"Two things," said Kent, "Fill me with breathless awe: the starry heavens and the moral law."

"I know a thing more awful and obscure," said Markam, "the long, long patience of the plundered poor."

Peace be with you, Jim.

What begins as a harangue by Tim against the absurdities and petty injustices of modern life morphs into a full-bodied press against church policies that elevate ruler and regulation over human compassion.

And another thing that bugs me is...

I t's time this sober periodical had a few obscene stories to spice up its Forum pages. Too often, *NCR's* pages are filled with only soft core disagreement on social and religious issues that really don't knock the wind out of us the way a good obscene story can.

As a writer, I am licensed to collect stories about which I might be tempted to comment. These, however, are free-standing storyettes that require little or no comment—only varying degrees of revulsion.

I found the first one in *NCR's* own Addenda column. It reported that Coleco Industries of West Hartford, Connecticut, will market a Rambo doll based on Sylvester Stallone's famous human destruction machine. Coleco's flack people have assured prospective buyers that the doll will come with "weaponry and vehicles, all things that create a proper play environment."

To go with your Coleco Rambo doll, the Wrigley gum people are marketing a Rambo Black Flak bubble gum—a black raspberry-flavored gum, shaped to resemble shrapnel or flak, and packed in a Rambo-emblazoned foil pouch.

Some kids may not want something as anemic as Rambomania products. If war is to be really fun, a kid needs a "Nukie," a plump little velvet thermonuclear warhead that you can buy in Winter Park, Florida, for only $50 a blast. Serious warmongers can build their own nuclear arsenal. And, when the kids to go bed, parents can have a wonderful time tossing the bomb around with the neighbors.

The marketing genius behind the cute Nukie says he's doing it "to get people to look at the humorous side of nuclear war."

For the more cerebral warmonger, a respected mail-order house will sell you for $155 a mounted collection of "bullets that shaped American history." Here, in a handsome frame, you can view replicas of bullets used at Lexington, Gettysburg and Little Bighorn—everything from musket balls to M-16s. No red-blooded American home should be without one.

These are free-standing storyettes that require little or no comment—only varying degrees of revulsion.

For capital punishment buffs, there's fun to be had at executions. A recent story in the *Chicago Sun-Times* describes the tailgate parties outside prisons on execution nights—parties complete with fireworks, lawn chairs and buckets of beer. After the bars close in Huntsville, Texas, on execution nights, students from Sam Houston State University go to the prison, carrying signs with rib-tickling messages to the condemned that say "This Bud's for you." Recently, when the attorney general announced that one condemned man had received a last-minute reprieve, the tailgaters booed.

Incidentally, you can get a guaranteed laugh with a neat little miniature electric chair that's ideal for your office. Just touch the seat and you get a zippy little jolt (batteries not included). A number of state officials are said to favor them.

I wonder whether people like that have battery-powered quartz clocks at home with the twelve apostles illustrating the twelve hours? Do they send their kids to school with Christian lunch bags? ("Take the Lord to lunch. Get God back in the schools.") Do they insist that their kids skate at the Christian roller rink or encourage them to listen to Christian bird calls or go on a Christian diet? All these I spotted recently and find faintly obscene.

Maybe we've got some dirt from the Holy Land, "the very soil on which he walked." I don't know what Holy Land dirt does for anyone—except to make ones house dirtier.

During a visit to Washington recently, I learned that the problem of those homeless men living on the street grates, which provide a measure of warmth on cold nights, has been addressed. A shelter, you ask? No, a more practical solution. They've covered up the grates.

The New York Times reports that the General Accounting Office in Washington has found that three-fifths—60 percent—of the Reagan administration officials receiving home/office limousine service are not authorized to have such service. Reagan likes to point his fingers at those "welfare Cadillacs." Now I know what he is talking about.

And then there's Mr. Edwin Meese, the attorney general. Almost everything he says is obscene. The high-level language that couches his prepared speeches appears almost conciliatory. He speaks glowingly of the "intent of the Constitution" as if to imply that his interpretation echoes that intent. At the functional level, it appears to be an effort to expand the privileges of the powerful and reduce the rights of the poor. One really doesn't have to be a lawyer these days to predict how a case will go from the attorney general's desk. Just one look at his In and Out box: the poor go in jail and the rich stay out.

A state prison—sadly, I missed the name—has a novel way of

sorting prisoners. Gay prisoners and those with a history of mental illness are dressed in different colored uniforms for easier identification. Think of it as a kind of Scarlet Uniform.

I can't pin this one down, but it comes from a second- or third-level bureaucrat. The topic was abused women, and his remark was, "Most of them are just bored housewives looking to get out."

Obscenities tend to attach themselves to institutions rather than individuals. Is it Peter or Parkinson who says once an organization reaches a certain size, it will tend to serve its own ends rather than the people it is supposed to serve? When this happens, obscenities occur. Some examples follow.

> Obscenities tend to attach themselves to institutions rather than individuals.

My friend Mike got a scare not long ago. The doctor told him his porch light was flickering and that he might consider eternity as a viable option. Mike is not married in the church, because his wife of twenty years was married before. He asked to see a priest, and the servant of God came with a message that if Mike wanted absolution, he'd have to "give up that woman." Mike did get well, no thanks to the priest. And next time, he's going to call direct. Jesus will understand.

The Vatican has issued a 28-page document called "A Proposed Schema for a Pontifical Document on Catholic Universities." It's a "put the wagons in a circle" document, and it will require that church authorities approve anyone who teaches theology in those institutions. That will about do it for the credibility of Catholic universities. Theology will drop back to graduate catechism and the better theologians will move to nonsectarian universities.

Canon 751 is mildly obscene in that it says obstinate doubt about some truth that must be believed with divine and Catholic faith partakes of heresy and could get one excommunicated. I've got some obstinate doubts on the wall of my mind that won't go away. I could lose my membership card.

The new code of canon law is an improvement on the old. It repeatedly urges pastoral approaches to the legal entanglements that a complex institution can find itself in. But it remains mildly obscene in that it clings to power in a way that would leave Jesus in the office waiting room of any chancery office. Power has its roots in fear, and fear leads to repression. The canons should be encouraging. They remain rather discouraging.

Finally, one can always find obscenities about how priests treat one another. It is a goal of each priest to seek perfection. But, all too often, the perfection sought is that of the institution rather than the person.

A priest left and married rather than lead a dishonest life with an honest woman. He has applied for permission to marry, but the Vatican continues to turn him down for "insufficient reason." Now he is dying of cancer and his wife has asked about a church burial. She's been told that he doesn't have a chance.

Now, this particular diocese has put people in consecrated ground who were so notoriously and openly bad that the flowers for acres around died instantly.

Why must a man's relationship with God flow through a fuse box with such low-amp circuit breakers? A good man is going home. But a chancery switch-man, instead of acting like a loving father or brother, must set limits and conditions. The switchman-priest just can't operate unless he is "in" and the others are "out."

Why is it that a church founded by a man who walked on water is now often administered by mean, mindless men who walk on the manure of guilt and betrayal and who prefer to flay consciences rather than to read the book of John? It's awfully hard to subordinate one's love of God to the rules of earthly ministers.

Well, that's enough. My injustice collection box is empty. I only wish that, after a decent interval, I could go back and find it still empty—with no Pauline scowl or Petrine fist under its lid.

I had hoped that the anger had gone out of the church and that, since Vatican II, it had become a softer, warmer place. I like a more confused, more forgetful church that leaves the lights on and the door open, and buries its dead with love and understanding.

This tribute to nuns produced an avalanche of supportive comments and
love letters from NCR readers. My heart is singing!" said one. "Just read
Unsworth on nuns and how right he is." Wrote another, "A copy of the
article should be sent to all the bishops in the country."

In praise of my sister and her sisters

In New York, a play about a looney nun who explained it all to you like Dr. Ruth drew lots of sophisticated New Yorkers, who normally get their jollies at plays about people who have sewer covers on their ids. Meanwhile, just off Broadway, two nuns run a place where homeless women can sleep for a few hours and find some food for their empty bellies.

In Chicago, a movie about a zoned-out nun who allegedly had a baby enjoyed a good run, but a few miles away a Daughter of Charity quietly asked a child-beater to put down a gun while the two seminarians with her ran like hell.

At a university cocktail party, a thrice-married history prof whose excesses with women are exceeded only by his devotion to the bottle blames his elementary school sisters who hit him on the knuckles with a ruler. Meanwhile, a patient nun at a nearby retreat house patches up the women who marry losers like this sot.

At the chancery of a good-sized diocese, a courageous nun informed the bishop that she was joining Alcoholics Anonymous. The bishop said she could join but would not be permitted to attend meetings because "it would set a bad example." She went to the meetings.

In Rome, higher clergy whose laundry is done by nuns worry about containing sisters who wish to decide the shape and content of their lives. Back in the United States, while a squad of sisters operate a home for unwanted, retarded children, the local Catholic paper prints letters from brittle Catholics who bemoan the fact that the sisters aren't wearing habits.

Nuns are getting a bad rap everywhere. They are objects of ridicule in those growing-up-Catholic books. Some former nuns write unbalanced books that suggest that convents are lesbian hives and mother superiors are S and M practitioners.

> In Rome, higher clergy whose laundry is done by nuns worry about containing sisters who wish to decide the shape and content of their lives.

A gay Catholic or a whiskey priest gets a fairer shake in the Catholic press than a nun. Many diocese publications will check the level of acceptance of a particular congregation of nuns with Rome before writing anything about them. Bishops rarely open their mouths about nuns other than to wish them happy anniversary and urge them to adhere to the goals of their foundress. Translation: get back into your habits and back on your stools.

It wasn't as bad when Ingrid Bergman and Audrey Hepburn were nuns. They brought a certain level of competence to their roles. Today, it seems, sisters rarely get a balanced image in any media.

Sure, some nuns are barely able to wash dishes competently. However, as a group, they have been and remain among the most talented and well-educated people in America. For the most part, everyone who came within the shadow of their habits was moved up at least one peg on life's ladder.

Sure, some nuns are nuts. But the overall nut level is, I believe, lower than the nut level of comparable groups.

> ≈ Nuns draw criticism because they generally do not approach issues from the point of view of power.

Nuns are perfect targets. It's easy to search our compulsive little egos and find some emotional pegs that won't go back in their proper bungholes. We all have at least one emotional tent flap waving in the breeze. It's convenient to transfer the blame to someone who cannot answer back. We can take a real or imagined hurt from our injustice box and blame our failure to deal with it maturely on some nun with a funny name who told us we would go to hell for wasting paper.

There are 118,000 nuns in the United States. That's a lot of Christians working to spread the Word. And the word they too often get back is one of ridicule.

Religious women may be the most innovative department of the church to come out of Vatican II—not a bad accomplishment, because, although they always outnumbered priests two to one, the nuns invited to Vatican II could easily have gone home on a bicycle.

Nuns draw criticism because they generally do not approach issues from the point of view of power. When churchmen meet, the underlying issue on any agenda is always power. While men debate their two-layer items, women go to the heart of the matter, take many more risks and accomplish much more. As a result, the sisters are measurably further along in their thinking and doing—and this gets some miters askew.

My sister, the nun, goes to a lot of meetings. I can't pretend to understand what they're all about. (Ginny has a Ph.D. in Oriental History and tends to talk very FM.)

When we visit at Christmas, she will have spent the morning serving meals to poor people before coming to dinner. She has taught English to Vietnamese refugees in Hong Kong and has written a history text for Bahamian children during her years in Nassau. Last year, she fell off a truck in Bolivia and snapped her wrist. She was hitchhiking with some other nuns to visit a poor village. And when she's home in New York, she teaches history to college students who still value a liberal arts education.

Nearly 40 years ago, she joined a congregation that wore coal-scuttle bonnets and expressly forbade eating hot dogs. (More accurately, one could eat the bun and the dog, but one could not put the dog on the bun. It was un-nun like.) Now, God help us, she drives a car, dresses in K-Mart polyester, jogs and lives in a walkup apartment with a covey of other sisters who try to live lives that mean something to their fellow human beings. In four decades, she and her adopted sisters have come quickly, sensibly and creatively into the 20th century. But they have not been welcomed as they should.

At that pre-Christmas synod, they never got around to the role of women in the church. That meeting was really about power, and there wasn't time to get into much else.

Meanwhile, many congregations of nuns were putting their old-age security at risk by divesting, while dioceses remained silent about their investments. Nuns make moral choices. Churchmen often make moral speeches and pragmatic choices.

Well, I've said it, and I'm glad. I miss the blue serge and white linen of my former teachers. But let them wear what they want. And, I did get whacked unjustly for things I didn't do by nuns who had more children than the old lady who lived in the shoe. But I got away with much more than I got whacked for.

So, the next time you're with a bishop who talks about "the good sisters" or a pastor who sends a case of pop to the convent while he slurps Courvoisier, or the layman who didn't get a promotion and traces it to his fourth-grade teacher—tell them to wise up. There are nuns who will rise up on the last day from shallow graces in El Salvador, from leper colonies in the Pacific, from graveyards next to hospitals, orphanages, schools, retreat houses and universities—and they will shame us with their loving smiles while a just God smacks us on the knuckles with a ruler.

And now, heeeere's Timothy—April 4, 1986

Tim's popularity as a columnist spawned a modest, auxiliary career as a TV commentator in the Chicago area. His specialty was the Inspiration Minute late at night or early morning. But it's clear he had no delusions of grandeur concerning his legacy before the camera.

My two minutes of fame

"Tim, we're trying to give laypeople a wider role in the church, and this little job will bring that objective closer. Would you give the Inspirational Minute on TV?"

I should have known better. Generally, any job passed from a collar to a necktie is normally best passed with rubber gloves. But John is an awfully nice priest and the prospect of being on TV, even for an inspirational 60 seconds, set some 200 pounds of libido quivering.

Television is a loose woman, sashaying into one's character. Unlike the Angelic Doctor, I had no flaming faggot with which to drive her away. Most likely, I'd have tossed the flaming faggot away anyway, and commenced the chase.

Saul had his thousands, I recalled. David had his ten thousands. No slight intended, but Tim would have his millions. My Breughel-like face would be beamed across five states. America's heartland would see and hear the Moses of the Midwest calling them to grace and contribution.

"Do four of them," John said. "They run them in the morning and night for about nine weeks, right after the 'Star Spangled Banner.' Then they do reruns. There will be four of you doing them—all faiths. Make them two minutes each."

Good Lord, what exposure! Not only was the Inspirational Minute actually two minutes, but it also meant that I'd be inspiring every fourth day for nine weeks, not counting the reruns. I figured it out to the nearest minute. I'd be on that tube 44 times with 88 Inspirational Minutes—and Fulton Sheen had been dead for nearly a decade.

I spent more time on the Inspirational Minute that I did on my will. They were a series of soft, elliptical sentences designed to go down like a slider from White Castle, a Midwest fast-food chain's tiny hamburgers that go down as if they were coated with Vaseline. I wasn't going to offend anyone the first time out. I'd save the fire and brimstone until I had my own show.

The long elevator ride to the studio was appropriate to my mood. I felt light in the loafers as I floated through the glass doors and announced myself to the wad of chewing gum at the reception desk.

I wanted her to think I was there to confront Bill Buckley, to take his big words and pompous thoughts into the shredder of my mind and reduce them to trail mix while telling him to sit up straight or I'd break his pedantic pencil over his pedantic head.

Alas, when I had to tell her that I was there for the Inspirational Minute, she pointed with *her* pencil.

The set was about the size of Chartres. Over in the corner was a lectern and a table with a vase of dusty plastic flowers. The camera was poised—a Cyclops with a red light on top that looked like an inflamed zit. No prompters. No guys with those big booms. This show had a lower budget than the installation of the first female bishop on the curia.

Three other Inspirational Minutemen were waiting. There was

a little rabbi who looked—well—just like a rabbi. The minister had about 63 teeth and looked healthier than a heretic had a right to be. The fourth guy was a wallie—you know, a person who is "off the wall," one of those guys who had discovered that God is a wet bird that does not fly at night. He had a theology formulated in a Veg-a-matic.

A fat guy in a folding chair was the only audience. He smoked a cigar while I delivered my sliders, his damnation assured.

The director was a pair of jeans and wire glasses. "When I make a fist," he said, "you've got 30 seconds to finish." (For this, he became a communications major?)

No retakes. No applause. It all took about as long as a bathroom break. It was a long ride back down that elevator.

But I had my schedule. In just a few weeks, my face would be as well-known as Garfield the Cat.

I was up at 4 a.m. on the morning of my first minute. I watched the test pattern for an hour to make certain that my eyes could discern every color. Seconds after the national anthem, I heard the gooey organ music and, suddenly, the TV camera was caressing the plastic flowers. In fact, I was 30 seconds into my Inspirational Minute before the camera moved from those damn flowers.

But at last, there I was—looking a little worse than the picture on my driver's license. My name was across my chest and my tie vibrated like the watered silk of a bishop's cincture. My sliders sounded a bit hurried, and before I got to the punch like, the camera was back on those phony flowers.

I thought I'd be mobbed when I got on the bus to go to work. I gave my seat to an old lady, thinking she would pass out with the shock of recognition. She thanked me and told me about her recent gall stone operation.

"Biggest stones the doctor ever saw," she said. "The doctor put my stones on TV in his classroom. Just imagine, I was on TV." I made her give the seat back.

At the university where I worked, I went into the cafeteria for my morning coffee. I expected it to be lined with palms. The short-order lady spotted me and asked, "Say, didn't I see you on TV this morning?" I beamed. At last, my inspirational arrow had found a target.

My Inspirational Minute might as well have been the morning pork-belly forecast. I could have fed all those who heard me with one loaf and two fishes.

"Well, yes," I said humbly. "That was me."

"I thought so," she said. "I was just putting on my brace. I've got a bad back, you know. Are you one of those running for judge?"

That was it. No one else said anything. My Inspirational Minute might as well have been the morning pork-belly forecast. I could have fed all those who heard me with one loaf and two fishes.

As the reruns began, a few others spotted me. An insomniac prof fell asleep in his chair one night only to awaken in time for my minute. He fell asleep again before my minute was up.

A couple caught me—or rather I caught them—late one night. They were otherwise engaged when she screamed, "Good Lord, it's Tim!" The next day, her husband told me what I had done to his inspirational minute and what I could do with mine.

Another couple learned of the incident. The new fans turned in the next night only to catch the wallie—the guy who thought God was the Green Hornet. They thought I had hooked in with those guys who dance at airports and stopped inviting me over for their yogurt pie and swamp-grass parties.

After a while, I stopped watching. The Inspirational Minute had lost its inspiration. No producer called. No fan mail came. Job didn't even send a card.

The next time around, the Roman Catholic church chose a red-cheeked young priest with tinted glasses who looked like St. Jerome's lion.

The Catholic church isn't ready for a dynamic leadership by lay-people. It will take a Vatican III. When they are ready, I'll be there.

After all, I've been on television 44 times.

Tim rarely devoted a whole column to satire. But in this classic from 1986 he brought his rapier to an imaginary diocese and its official directory. As it turned out, he wasn't just having fun, he was cutting close to the bone.

Pardon my correction

This memorandum was culled from the files of the Very Human Church:

TO: All diocesan offices, parishes, schools agencies
FROM: Ms. Sukey Boxley, Administrative assistant to the Most Reverend Fursey Bodkin, Bishop of Exodus, MO.
RE: Corrections to the Diocesan Directory

Our apologies for the late appearance of the annual Diocesan Directory. The manuscript was temporarily lost in the trunk of Bishop Bodkin's car, under Bishop Bodkins's model of the all-purpose parish center under construction at St. Zealot's.

Please make the following changes in your '86 Directory:

Page 3: Auxiliary Bishop Most Reverend Titus Frisbie, DD, is not the titular bishop of Gezer. Bishop Frisbie is the titular Bishop of Hazor. (Bishop Frisbie informs that Bishop Leroy Hamper is titular Bishop of Gezer and that Bishop Frisbie's titular see is twice as big as Bishop Hamper's. Bishop Frisbie further informs that he was not amused when he was introduced at a recent Confirmation liturgy as "the old geezer from Gezer.")

Page 4: The Right Reverend Plunket Plummer should have the designation "P.A." after his name. It denotes "protonotary apostolic" and permits him to pontificate four times each year. As such, he should be listed above the Right Reverend Ignatius Dooley, who is only a Domestic Prelate and, as such, cannot pontificate.

Page 7: Reverend William E. Spraggs, associate pastor, St. Lumen's Church—DELETE. (Also, page 21, Sister Charity Andrews of the same parish's elementary school—DELETE.)

Page 9: Reverend Luke Connolly, pastor emeritus, Holy Grail Parish, is no longer in residence. He is now completely retired and living in Bountiful, Florida. His address and telephone number are unlisted at his request. (Father advises that other clergy visiting Florida can find readily available motels.)

Page 11: Father Urban Spiegal's congregation designation is OSB—not SOB, as reported. (Miss Boxley regrets this error, but insists that she asked Bishop Bodkin what Father Spiegal was. Bishop Bodkin regrets the error and states that it has nothing to do with Father Spiegal's remark from the pulpit that the bishop could not break ladies par.)

Page 28: Sister Veronica Joiner, CSJJ, is no longer the DRE at St. Viator's. She is now the executive director of the Coalition to Unite All Coalitions.

Page 42: The Fathers of the Precious Blood of Jesus and Mary, commonly known as "The Bleeders," are now called the Discernment Fathers.

Page 48: The Slaves of Our Lady of Goyim, whose motherhouse is in the Diocese of Exodus, are now known as the Sisters of the Inclusive

Language. (Bishop Bodkin, however, stated that he will continue to regard them as the Slaves.)

Page 61: The sacramental records of St. Jarlath's Parish, which was closed during the past year, are not at St. Ita's, as reported. Unfortunately, they were accidentally shredded when the pastor, Father Gaulbert Dobbins, was destroying the parish's financial records. (*The Exodus Trumpet* will publish a statement in due time about the status of these now unrecorded sacraments. Couples who were married at St. Jarlath's should refrain from all marital acts until a ruling is received from the Sacred Roman Rota.)

Page 71: Stanley Pulaski, permanent deacon, St. Casmir Parish, informs that his wife's name is Wanda, not Anne, as reported. (This office has learned that Anne was the name of his first wife. DELETE both Stanley and Wanda.)

Page 81: We sincerely regret the omission of the entire Class of 1968 from the ordination class listings. (The error occurred when the Directory secretary, Sukey Boxley, overheard Bishop Bodkin remarking to the Chancellor, "Hell, there's nobody in the '68 class.")

Page 96: The office of the Opus Dei Prelature is no longer in the basement of 881 Flogme Lane, the bishop's mansion. The office is now in the lower level of the lighthouse on Lake Megiddo. (It was relocated when the bishop discovered that his answering machine had a second tape recorder attached to it.)

Page 111: The Directory apologizes to the McClatchey Brothers Funeral Home for the incorrect telephone listing in their display. The number given was that of the Original Cohen Brothers Funeral Parlor. (Our sincere apologies to the Gage and Dillon families, whose loved ones were buried from Temple Achsaph. Bishop Bodkin is now negotiating with Rabbi Blintz for the release of the Christians.)

Page 114: Please ignore or remove the advertisement for the Available Light Book Center. The diocese has returned its payment for the display. At the time the diocese agreed to print the ad, it was unaware that they carried books by Curran, Küng and McBrien. Bishop Bodkin stated that the Exodus Diocese does not endorse books by heretics, especially heretics who are not humble.

Page 116: Please delete the title "Very Reverend" from the Reverend Milton Lubash's listing. (N.B.: This is not a clerical error. Father Lubash entered the designation himself on his computerized questionnaire. Bishop Bodkin informs that Father Lubash is a "nothing."

Kindly send additional corrections to: Sukey Boxley, Diocese of Exodus, P. O. Box 39, Exodus, MO 33178. Please do not call. Sometimes, Bishop Bodkin answers the phone himself and he does not like to take correction over the phone.

A sort of spotty portrait of priests we all know
—September 4, 1987

Tim seems never to have met a priest he didn't like. Though not one himself, he had a unique ability to get inside a priest's heart and mind. His respect for their calling was huge, and so was his ear for their quirkiness. Remember, this was written before any of us had any idea of the extent of the pedophilia crisis, which hurt Tim greatly. But still, he has maintained his admiration for the great majority of priests and bishops.

Bless me, Father...

I can't recall when I've had a bad conversation with a priest. Perhaps that's because I get to pick my priests. But I don't think so.

It's largely because priests are really nice guys—well-educated, generally well-read, unheralded idealists, caring and prayerful men who still love God and neighbor as much as they did when they prostrated themselves in the sanctuary on ordination day.

Recently, a clerical friend asked me to put down some thoughts on priests. It was part of a continuing dialogue on priestly morale, life quality and such. I made some notes and culled others from items I had tossed in a file marked "priests." Like a Seurat painting, they are a pattern of pure color dots. Together, they might create a kind of clerical pointillism.

- "Let's see, now. Three weeks from now, less two days, I'll be ordained 38 years." That's how the old guys used to go on, especially when they had a little drink taken. Now, however, what you hear is: "Let's see, now. Two weeks from today and I'll be just six months from retirement." Something's changed.

- Before the late great Monsignor Reynald Hillenbrand died, the renowned rector, teacher and writer was visited by one of his former students. "Did I do any good?" the old priest asked his protégé. "Did I do *any* good?" Today's priests are still asking themselves that question—only at a much earlier age.

- According to one reliable survey, more than 80 percent of parishioners like their parish priests. Politicians pray for an acceptance rate as good as that. The local butcher can only dream of such an approval level. Priests are programmed emotionally for approval rates that are higher than those Jesus got. Seminarians should be asked to build pedestals while in the seminary. Then, hold a liturgy and burn the damn things.

> ≋ Seminarians should be asked to build pedestals while in the seminary. Then, hold a liturgy and burn the damn things.

- I wonder what the clerical shortage would be like today if we could magically get back all those guys who were tossed out of the seminary for not being able to decline an irregular Latin verb?

- "There's no shortage of priests," a priest told me. "Only a shortage of imagination."

- In Tom Peter's book *Pursuit of Excellence*, he points out that policies should always be made for the best people. It seems to me clergy often make policies with their worst people in minds.

- Put another way, the clergy might just have to face the fact that a certain percentage of their people are simply unemployable.

- Try another way still. One priest, viewing the alleged clergy shortage, said, "Hell, we ought to fire at least 10 percent of what we've got. We'd be a lot better off."

- "I talked to my married brother," another priest said. "And he told me that the grass *is* greener. Sure, the crap's the same in or out of the priesthood. It's celibacy that makes the difference. It leaves us all off center."

- Priests whose pants never reach their shoe tops always wear white socks.

- Priests are funny. They get praise and it makes them feel good. But criticism makes them feel worse than praise makes them feel good. A pity. A lot of low self-concepts. But, then, I know a bishop who gets spooked by *The Wanderer*.

- When Ron called the chancery, he was excited about the neat idea he had for raising the heat level of the faithful in his parish. The bishop's vicar listened and said, "Sounds exciting. Let me get back to you." Two days later, the chancery cleric called back and said, "Ron, we think you'd better put your idea on hold for a while. We've gotta protect the boss and maybe this idea wouldn't wash." So Ron's spark is watered and his parishioners go hungry.

- Priests work where the tire meets the pavement. When they convey such street-level experiences to a chancery priest, it is heard very differently. It's easier to just do it and apologize after, said one shrewd priest.

- How come the ads for directors of religious education (DREs) list qualifications just short of the Nobel Prize? But there are no professional qualifications or evaluations for priests. If priests were evaluated, then the overall quality would improve; some of the better ones who resigned might return; some of the weak ones would leave and lighten the burden for the others. However, priests will fight evaluation just as some teachers, most judges and all politicians do.

- Priests affect their parishioners about as much as *they* are affected by *them*.

- Seriously, would *you* really want to spend "16 glorious days" visiting the Catholic theme parks of Europe with one of the priests in those travel ads?

> Priests who lead dangerous lives are tremendously life-giving and affirmative.

- Priests who lead dangerous lives are tremendously life-giving and affirmative.

- A lot of low-radiation and anti-clericalism would disappear if clergy would be more attentive to their social obligations. Virtually every working person holds a job in which a failure to appear on schedule, a last minute cancellation, or even neglecting to return a phone call can get one in Very Big Trouble. However, too many priests do all these things with impunity. The common excuses are that they're busy with other things or their time is not their own. Such excuses just don't stand examination. The syndrome starts in the seminary. Let seminarians de-emphasize other things and emphasize these obligations. Mies van der Rohe used to say, "God is in the details."

• "Have patience; have hope," the bishop said to one of the young priests in his diocese. "Go on with your work. I can't support you publicly, but as long as you're prudent I won't stop you." Thus groweth the number of conspiracies between a caring bishop and his priests so that the work of God can go on undetected by the ecclesial structure.

• The clergy are having fewer parties these days. That's a shame. There ought to be more parties—more nights to sit around and gossip, criticize, tell jokes, overeat and vent. I'm hearing that young priests in particular aren't meeting as much as they used to. A pity. It weakens the warm soft chains that bind them together.

• Bill read the letter from the chancery in which the Vatican said that those group reconciliation services had to go. He read it to his parishioners and they talked about it for a long time. Finally, the people said, "Father, we need those services. They cure an awful lot of fear and loathing, and they've increased one-on-one confession." So Bill made a pastoral decision and the monthly service has continued. The chancery knows about it but doesn't want to touch it with a 10-foot crosier. In such matters, chanceries—and the curia—have only as much authority as an individual priest wants to give them.

• I think the number of careerist priests is dwindling. But they're still around, generally slowing the work of the others.

• George wasn't an inspiring speaker even before he took the homilitics workshop. Now, he speaks pure, unaccented foghorn.

TIM UNSWORTH

He uses slippery, calves' liver words like "visioning," "brainstorming," "surfacing issues," "energize," "prioritization," and "faith foundation." Pure pulpitspeak. George would have been better off hearing some solid theology lectures or getting into therapy to examine the roots of his fear of people. Foghorn language is designed to distance and control—not to communicate.

> I'd feel a little better about clericalism if I could see a priest on a city bus.

- A lot of clergy are going around without their clericals. That's fine with me, although some priests should keep in mind that black does have a certain slimming effect. More important, if a priest prefers mufti, let him do better than one of those knit shirts and baggy, black pants. Priests should get a decent jacket, slacks, shirt and tie. They should check out European clergy. Or dress like Charlie Curran or Richard McBrien—not like someone on a work-release program. Otherwise, they should wear the black.

- I don't know why, but I'd feel a little better about clericalism if I could see a priest on a city bus.

- "Damn it," the priest said. "I almost wish that we'd go back to the old days with all the secrecy. Back then, at least, when Rome issued a document, it went to the bishop first. He read it and then called a secret meeting of priests who could develop a pastoral response or some teaching protocols. Then the regular clergy got it and we still had time to prepare before telling the people. Now we hear nothing from the bishop. We get the text in *The New York Times*. If the bishop has something to say, he calls a press conference and talks to the media. No wonder we feel left out."

• Years ago, everyone bitched when the pastor moved his spinster sister into the rectory to be the housekeeper and the parish wiretap. Not ideal, but at least it gave the old buffalo a sense of family. Now that many rectories are becoming single-occupancy houses, it might be a good idea to move the pastor's sister and her whole family into the rectory. At least, the Lone Ranger pastor would have some sense of family, and his sister's kids would bring some life to the place.

• The three homosexual, celibate seminarians asked a favored prof, "We want to announce that we are homosexual and celibate and that we want to remain in priestly ministry. What do you suppose would happen?" "You'd be kicked out," he answered. "Because we're homosexual?" they asked. "No," he said, "because you're crazy."

• I asked a priest friend who works in a chancery, "Who will the new auxiliary bishop be?" "I haven't the faintest idea," he said. "No one even speculates. They all want the job themselves."

• In spite of the fact that a lot of authoritarian structures have lessened considerably, the gap between the bishop and the lower clergy hasn't narrowed much at all. Nice guys. But very different agendas.

• On Chicago's Michigan Avenue, there are clusters of elite private clubs. They are wonderful, old collegiate gothic structures with brass doors and worn doorsteps—places where members are addressed by their surnames and the attendants are addressed by their first names. There's a kind of elegant tackiness about them. It would remind one of churches. The clubs are slowly dying. The city's movers and shakers, who know how to run their enterprises, just don't want their clubs changed. So women, blacks, Jews—even Catholics—are often denied membership. The clubs are now objects of ridicule and anger, and people are seeking alternative places. Not many years hence, the old tombs will be little more than footnotes to this nation's social history. The resemblance to clericalism is frightening.

- Recently, I listened to a priest talking about Mary in Scripture. He was outstanding. In a world where so many talkers speak with their mouths and not with their hearts, it was a moving experience. All priests are ordained to speak from their hearts. That's what makes them unique and terribly important.

> All priests are ordained to speak from their hearts. That's what makes them unique and terribly important.

- An honest priest is never permanently lonely or discontented.

- Dan Cantwell is a saint. He's a monsignor, a title he terms "ridiculous." He says, "Groping, not pontificating, is the church I know and love. Moving, not standing still, a church on the move! I see the church not as something over against the world but as breath of the world. It liberates from pettiness, smallness, despair. It revels in friendship, love and eating together.... The world does not need redemption; our hearts and minds do."

• One can quote Dan Cantwell by the yard. Unvarnished. Unfiltered. He's in his seventies now and, while other priests calcify and pray that their prostate gland will stay put, Dan asks, "What surprises are in store for us? Is the church of the future already coming into being at the grass roots?"

• After my pastor was ordained in 1949, he returned to the seminary to pick up his things and get a final retreat before setting out on his first assignment. After a week of ordination celebrations, he found he couldn't sleep. So he took a walk on the seminary's vast, dark grounds. Walking from building to building, he met Mike, the immigrant Irish night watchman. They chatted a bit and, just as they parted, Mike tipped his hat and said, "Good night, Father." "I can't remember anything from my ordination retreat or much of anything from my ordination mass and the ones that followed that week," the priest told me. "But for the past 38 years, I've been trying to live up to what Michael McDevitt said to me that night."

Good night, Fathers.

In this column, Tim made a personal argument for optional celibacy. He noted how diligently the bishops sought widespread opinion and testimony before writing their major pastoral letters on peace and the economy, and he wondered why this issue involving the strongest emotion in our bodies is dictated from the top down.

Celibacy is robbing us of the priests we need and want

George Bernanos' sensitive and compassionate novel, *The Diary of a Country Priest*, is 52 years old this year—about the age of the average priest.

The Diary has stood the test of time. It now qualifies as literature. It's a great novel, one that combines simplicity with insight. It deserves another reading, if only to confirm the axiom that the more things change the more they remain the same.

Perhaps the only difference between today's priest and the diarist is that the lonely priest in *The Diary* says, "Naturally, I keep those thoughts to myself. But I am not ashamed of them." Today, it seems, clergy are encouraged not to have an unexpressed thought. If it can't be said at an overnight retreat at the seminary or a Crystal Cathedral healing session, there's always the Phil Donahue show. (Come to think of it, Bernanos' priest did *not* keep it to himself. It's all there. Priestly clay is priestly clay.)

"Our superiors," the diarist writes, "are no longer official optimists. Those who still profess the rule of hope, teach optimism only by force of habit, without believing what they say."

Was *that* half a century ago?

≈ Will bishops be forced to continue to search for a credible theology of celibacy while closing their eyes and even indirectly supporting the abuses?

When I was in Rome last October, hanging around outside the doors of the synod with the rest of the laity, I was told that the punch list for Episcopal candidates was growing longer and longer and that many thoughtful and honest candidates had to quietly turn the purple down because they couldn't, in good conscience, support universal celibacy or turn their backs on women. Those who pass scrutiny today can only widen the rowing gap between supporters of company policy and the lived experience of the priest who functions where the tire meets the street. The official color has turned to bland, tinged with ambition.

Are we going to become like the church of France? Recent surveys indicate that only about four percent of the Catholic French are mass-going. Will American priests become antiquated objects of ridicule? Allegedly, France now has 20,000 priestless parishes. There are not quite 20,000 parishes in the United States, but about 1,000 of them are now said to be without resident priests.

Will bishops be forced to continue to search for a credible theology of celibacy while closing their eyes and even indirectly supporting the abuses? Is the underlying issue not celibacy but control, i.e., would the Vatican rather tolerate a 50 percent reduction in its ranks before the turn of the century than lose the control they think they enjoy under the current discipline?

It's reasonable to assume the church could tolerate celibate homosexuals among its clergy so long as the numbers reflected society as a whole—10 percent—but can a mixed celibate group function effectively when 35 to 50 percent of its numbers have a homosexual orientation?

But I'm wandering. In *The Diary*, the young priest visits the Curé de Tercy, an uninspiring but street-wise priest with enough clout and self-confidence to be able to turn away the various purveyors the bishop sends to his parish to peddle their poor quality goods—an action conceptually akin to throwing diocesan directives concerning altar girls into the basket:

> I'm wondering what you've got in your veins these days, you young priests! When I was your age we had *men* in the church…men I say—heads of a parish, masters, my boy, *rulers*. They could hold a whole country together, that sort could—with a mere lift of the chin. Oh, I know what you're going to say: they fed well, drank good wine and didn't object to a game of cards. Well, what of it? When you tackle your job properly, you get through it quickly and efficiently, there's plenty of time left over, and it's all the better for everybody.
>
> Nowadays, the seminarians turn out little choirboys, little ragamuffins who think they're working harder than anybody because they never get anything done. They go sniveling around instead of giving orders. They read stacks of books but never…understand what it means when we say that the church is the bride of Christ…. The mistake she (the church) made wasn't to fight dirt…but to try to do away with it altogether. As if that were possible!… A real housewife knows that her home isn't a shrine. Those are just poets' dreams.

Good God, has nothing changed?

There are few things my wife Jean and I enjoy more than having a priest or two over for dinner. It's always a good chew of the fat. They are gentle men, articulate, well-read, witty, good storytellers, good listeners. They are men who don't expect "jam" on their priesthood, as the old pastor in *The Diary* puts it. We are always enriched by their presence.

But of late we are saddened by what we see and hear. We see so much weariness.

Peter had nine funerals in one week. Andrew must endure a pastor who is a drunk and keeps a smelly dog. James must take sick calls in a neighboring parish because that pastor simply ignores them.

Some are bitter. They see so much compromise in the name of preserving the structure. Others are troubled by the civil war—one wag called it the Trojan War—among the bishops over a single paragraph in a thoughtful pastoral on a plague-threatening issue.

John witnesses a pastor paying $350 a week from a parish fund to support a child he has fathered. Philip would like to take a woman to dinner but can't, lest he give scandal, although his homosexual colleagues in the ministry are free to enjoy one another's company in public or in the rectory.

Bartholomew wonders aloud why the vast majority of priests are tarred with the same brush because known pederasts are not disciplined and treated until the state attorney makes a call. Matthew has ended a serious relationship with a good woman and retreated into prayer and jogging. Another James wants to apply for a challenging pastorate but has been told that a third-string assistant priest comes with the appointment. Thaddeus is trying to find a way to retire at 60. Simon learns that a sensitive petition he submitted through the bureaucracy has been altered to protect another man's career. Matthias, an inner-city pastor, hears from a colleague that a mutual friend is in line for a "significant" parish (as opposed to what?).

So it goes. A lot of good guys with broken wings.

We see good priests on the steps of the various churches we visit. They can work the back of the church better than a squad of presidential candidates. They are often in the cold—not even a coat over their vestments—greeting parishioners and trading in the small change of post-liturgy conversation. We see them in the hospitals, visiting parishioners, and we watch them clean out purgatory by enduring endless meetings on issues that are inversely proportional to the length of the meeting.

Studies show they are almost universally liked by their parishioners. The majority are people-centered and caring. They are bound together by what John Shea calls "a covenant of the spirit." In their presence, to cite Shea again, "the stirrings of our souls can have a hearing." Good men. They want the priesthood to work.

> Of late priests' energies are terribly drained by the need to carry the enormous burden of celibacy within an institutional environment that is almost bankrupt of emotional support to give its priests.

However, of late their energies are terribly drained by the need to carry the enormous burden of celibacy within an institutional environment that is almost bankrupt of emotional support to give its priests. There seems to be an unconscionable amount of time devoted to maintaining a discipline that the majority do not want.

It's troubling to note that the methodology for developing a theology for framing a response to nuclear weapons, labor, poverty and economic issues is always from the bottom up. For the economic pastoral, they practically interviewed Mary and Joseph's donkey. But issues involving the strongest emotion in our bodies are dictated from the top down.

"Make all pastors bishops," one cynical priest suggested. "That would solve the problem." At least these virtually powerless men would have some power. It may be as good an answer as any these days.

>≈≈ The issues surrounding priesthood and its biggest problem—celibacy—are being handled as if a Bing Crosby or Spencer Tracy culture were still the norm.

Dean Hoge's careful study of the priest shortage, *The Future of Catholic Leadership*, establishes without doubt that the vocation shortage is long-term and that the church is powerless to reverse it. Further, Hoge's research reveals that the shortage of priests is an institutional problem, not a spiritual one. Yet, the issues surrounding priesthood and its biggest problem—celibacy—are being handled as if a Bing Crosby or Spencer Tracy culture were still the norm.

Even as I reread *The Diary,* I am plowing through an altar-missal-sized history of the Sears Company, *The Big Store*, by Donald R. Katz. It carries the same shock of recognition as *The Diary*.

"Inside Sears," the corporate biographer writes, "I found brilliant managers, awful managers, great tellers of jokes, selling fools, natural merchants, operators, computer geniuses, wheeler-dealers, hatchet men, martinets, victims, sycophants, patricians, good old boys and ghosts.

"Senior Searsmen (read bishops) were trained from their corporate infancy to participate in a veritable cult of contrived harmony and consensus...disagreement was fine; sustained discord was anti-Sears. You were supposed to 'go along' with things in line with a tradition."

Ed Telling, the CEO who brought Sears back to life, gave a commencement speech in which he spoke of two powerful and competing traditions within institutions:

> On the one hand, there is the largely British tradition of Hume, Adam Smith and Burke which held that the basic function of government was simply to provide a framework within which the creative powers of all the people would be free to operate.... The continental vision of Voltaire, Rousseau and Descartes [he could have added Aquinas], on the other hand held that man...could lay out the blueprint of the good society and that government should be used to achieve and implement what pure reason declared to be good.

The citation defines the cleavage between the American tradition and the Vatican one. "The company I represent," Telling added, "with its thousands of different items of merchandise, epitomizes the richness and diversity which can develop only when a central authority does *not* dictate."

Someone should declare the Sears history a pastoral letter and mail it to the Vatican.

In Rome, during the first week of the recent synod, I met a priest from a rural, one-priest parish. He was traveling for three months. After a few sentences each, I began to suspect that this man's cheese was slipping off his cracker. "Who's looking after the store, Father?" I asked. "Oh, everything's fine," he said. "I consecrated 4,000 hosts before I left."

That poor wacko survives by playing it by the book. His porch light is nearly out, but he represents the observant church.

One hurting priest said, "Only after we're down to one priest saying mass on satellite TV for the whole damn world will the church change its teaching on celibacy."

I hope not. But maybe—just maybe—the entire clerical culture, right down to its La-Z-Boy chairs, Formica desks and baggy black pants, has to disappear before real change can come.

"Oh, I don't accuse these people of hypocrisy; I believe them to be sincere. So many of us, supposedly standing for law and order, are merely clinging on to old habits, sometimes to a mere parrot vocabulary, its formulae worn so smooth by constant use that they justify everything and question none" (*The Diary of a Country Priest*).

The oils have dried but friendship lingers—July 19, 1991

In a reprise and critique of the seminary system once popular with many large dioceses in the 20th century, Tim showed how the system began to fall apart in the 1960s. Quigley, the minor seminary mentioned here, was finally closed to become the offices for the Archdiocese of Chicago in 2008.

Should auld acquaintance be forgot?

At the silver anniversary reunion of Chicago's St. Mary of the Lake Seminary class of 1966, 38 priests—19 active, 19 resigned—gathered at a conference center in Itasca, Illinois, to celebrate. (Later, a liturgical celebration was held at the Mundelein Seminary to celebrate their ordination. Only the active priests were formally invited, however. The authorities felt that the presence of resigned priests would throw the current seminarians off balance. They remain intent upon keeping their baby clerics safe from emotional maturity.)

In 1954, 276 barely-pubescent boys entered Quigley Preparatory Seminary, a day school that may have produced more lawyers, politicians and teachers than priests. "Only 10 percent of you will make it to ordination," they were told in the Marine Corps rhetoric that characterized the muscular church of that day. Other members of the class—called "specials"—entered later.

Almost 15 percent of the original group made it through the 12-year program. ("Any organization that spends 12 years training its people has gotta be neurotic," one priest observed.) But no one could ever have imagined that less than 7 percent would survive in active ministry to the class's silver anniversary, 37 years later.

Bob, now rector of Chicago's limestone cathedral, observed that the per-priest cost was terribly high. "But," he said, "a businessman friend of mine felt that $375,000 to educate someone who would work for him for 50 years at $12,000 a year wasn't a bad deal."

Seminary training was "incredibly impersonal" in those days, according to another classmate. "When I said that to the rector," the priest said, "he answered, 'What do you mean? We do your laundry.'"

The seminarians entered as spring steel, tempered and flexible. The system attempted to reheat them and pour them into iron molds. They received a better-than-average education, did work for their fellow Christians that was not aimed at messing up the world and forged friendships with one another that would endure. They griped about their rector and some of their profs and cheered when Jack Gorman, now a bishop, was named rector just before their ordination.

Each class had a nickname. Optimistically, the 1966 class members called themselves the "prophets." Like most isolated groups, they formed their own language. "Grease" was the universal part of speech used to describe any action or emotion.

They walked the huge property in their heavy capes—clerical Linus blankets called "zimarras"—which had been passed on from one seminarian to another until the black wool had literally turned green. The zimarras and birettas were part of the cult. Years later, they had the emotional pull of old school sweaters.

Forty-three were ordained for the Chicago church in 1966. Today, 19 remain on the active roster. In recent years, the average fallout rate from ordination to silver jubilee has been about 39 percent. But the 1966 class lost 56 percent.

Dan, a resigned member of the class, now executive director of Call to Action, said it was the influence of the Kennedys and Martin Luther King, Jr., the Vietnam War, civil rights, celibacy and birth control issues. "Oh, that's pure Dan," his friend Pat, now a criminal lawyer, said. "It may have been some of those things, but mostly it was burnout."

"I left in 1974," Pat said. "I felt I didn't want to be the guy to turn out the last vigil light. I was in a poor parish. We used to be able to go down to Catholic Charities and get some under-the-table money to keep the parish going. But it all got to be too much. I used to feel awful when a guy left. I'd have stomach cramps and I couldn't sleep. And then suddenly I left, too."

≈ There was reluctance on the part of those who stayed to contact those who left, and vice versa. The active men felt betrayed and abandoned; those who left sensed a lack of support.

Men left silently. "We felt awful," Joe, now a pastor in a Latino parish, recalled. "After all, we were told that these men were Judases."

There was reluctance on the part of those who stayed to contact those who left, and vice versa. The active men felt betrayed and abandoned; those who left sensed a lack of support. An erratic and dictatorial cardinal often gave resigned priests only 24 hours to clear out of their rectories.

Without any thought as to their preferences, the old system assigned priests to parishes. "We had no choice in those days," Tom, now pastor in a black community, said. "I was lucky in my first assignment, but some of the guys weren't. They were assigned to throwbacks."

By December 1968, four had resigned. Four more were gone by

May 1970. The remainder departed over the years—the most recent just months before their jubilee celebration, which he attended briefly with his fiancée.

Vatican II (1962-1965) was held during their final years of theology. "The ink was still wet on the documents," Tom recalled, "but we got them and arrived in parishes where the people hadn't heard of them and the old guard pastors were resisting active service." Today, Tom is vice president of a hospital and an active member of his parish, often conducting morning Eucharistic liturgies designed, ironically, to be used in the absence of a priest.

Tom took notes throughout the three-day reunion. He quoted Jim, an inner-city pastor, boasting cheerfully, "God is just crazy about me!" while others spoke with great candor that they had not found much nourishment in the church.

Those who remained in active ministry did not escape their problems. One thoughtful man acknowledged that he is "about 60-40" but still "hanging in there." One is still negotiating fruitlessly for an assignment within the diocese; another has had a priesthood marked by constant illness. Some resented their isolation in ethnic parishes; at least one had gone from liberal to conservative.

Most were pastors, but Bill, perhaps the most gifted man in the class, had steadfastly refused to become one. Ed runs the Extension Society, normally the training wheels for a bishopric; Charlie, an iconoclast, thrives on his work at Catholic Charities.

But no one got a free lunch. Life for those who stayed and those who left has been equally messy.

It was a close-knit class. Those who remained in ministry met almost every year. Resigned members were invited to the 20-year reunion but weren't entirely comfortable. By the 25th anniversary, the average priest had reached age 50. The experiences had brought them acceptance. No one wanted to break the bruised reed or extinguish the smoking flax.

Priests can out talk insurance salespeople. It was unfiltered stuff. Those who had resigned urged those who were still active to stay where they were.

"You're doing great work," they said to them. "Stay with it." But they were concerned about the downward spiral in which the active ones were caught—fewer priests, more parishioners, less money, more paperwork.

> Maybe the vaunted indelible mark of holy orders is really the oil of friendship.

It was a family reunion. Men who had not been that close during the seminary years became closer after years of separation. Once essentially shallow relationships were deepened. Thoughts once forbidden could be expressed because they were not hobbled by judgments. Priests could talk about pain.

Today, the entire high-school seminary in Chicago has fewer kids than the freshman class that entered Quigley 37 years ago. The major seminary has only a few more in the entire final four years than in this one ordination class. The new breed of seminarians are orchids. We'll just have to wait to see how they bloom.

I don't know what the reunion means. A second ordination, perhaps. Maybe the vaunted indelible mark of holy orders is really the oil of friendship.

Tim was powerfully attracted to underdogs, as his account of a gay and lesbian mass at a Chicago church showed. He was heartened by how they had gotten past their anger and—despite their disputes with the church—experienced grace and peace in the liturgy.

I wonder as I wander

The mass for gays and lesbians is held on Sunday nights in what was once a lace-curtain Irish parish just off the lakefront. It's a Tudor Gothic church—the kind you could build when stone-carvers earned 15 cents an hour.

Its organ can raise the hair on the back of your neck, and its dark-stained pews reach out and grab you. This church is no all-purpose liturgical rumpus room with an ironing board for an altar. It's for praying.

The gays began coming to this church when a nearby parish they used to attend burned down. Their former parish is now a parking lot with millions of prayers under its asphalt skin. So it goes.

Now, about 200 gay and lesbian Christians come to the great stone edifice to pray to a God who accepts them as they are. It probably took a lot of doing, especially with groups such as Dignity being banned from praying on church property all around the country.

I hear about the liturgy from a gay friend who is dying of AIDS and whose father, a doily communicant, won't visit him. The old man is getting fat on the Eucharist, but it isn't moving any of the rocks in his soul.

My wife Jean and I sat beneath Veronica Wipes the Face of Jesus, one of the huge stations that, however syrupy, still engage the imagination. (Just before he went to Fatima recently, John Paul II scratched Veronica from the stations. She isn't scriptural-based. I find that a great irony, since Veronica's act of mercy is more credible and more appealing to me than the visions of the three kids at Fatima. Veronica didn't shout, "Repent!" She recognized that life was messy and did what she could.)

The liturgy could have been a rerun of a 1950s seminary mass. It was easy to conjure up a high-ceilinged chapel filled with seminarians in regimental *soutanes*. It was muggier than a sumo wrestler's navel that night, and the gays, some of whom are given to dressing creatively, made me stretch a bit in the tolerance department. But their voices reminded me of a seminary choir.

> While other Catholics quit the church when they learn that the Round Robin game at the Friday night Bingo was rigged, these Catholics cling to the hem of garments that are being pulled away from them.

These Christians love one another. They come out to express their faith and their sexuality, two of the most difficult topics to talk about. They are miracles of faith—women and men who are attempting to find a pathway to sanctity through not only the strewn rocks in everyone's path but also through those that are thrown at them by their fellow Christians.

While other Catholics quit the church when they learn that the Round Robin game at the Friday night Bingo was rigged, these Catholics cling to the hem of garments that are being pulled away from them.

Many of the men were stereotypically gay: small-waisted, neatly groomed, trimly mustached and carefully dressed. But there were many others—older, full-bellied men who could have been the guys who come out when you ring the bell at the supermarket meat counter. They could have been my classmates.

Years ago, they could have attended the parish mission during Men's Week and heard the sweating priest fulminate on Sixth Commandment Night about sins so terrible that the heavens cry out for vengeance. "Unnatural!" the mission director yelled—a far greater sin than kissing Bernadette Moser in the rumble seat.

> I wonder what they might have achieved if they had not been lugging a cross of guilt all those years.

I wonder how these men felt when they were young and were told that they'd burn in hell until the place froze over. I wonder now why we didn't have Pharisee Night right after Sixth Commandment Night. I wonder how these now gray-haired men kept their faith through all those years, believing in the church that called them deviates. I wonder what they might have achieved if they had not been lugging a cross of guilt all those years.

I wonder how they felt when reading in the diocesan paper that the cathedral doors were opened for the annual lawyers' or politicians' mass, during which the presiding prelate heaped praise on the heads of people who were most likely passing each other brown envelopes during the liturgy.

I wonder how the gays felt when they read of the more than 1,000 wiseguys in Chicago who have passed away in the trunks of cars since 1929 and had their sins bathed in holy water before being buried in church cemeteries called something like "Gate of Heaven."

But I shouldn't wonder. These gays I talked to about this mass had no such sarcastic views. Although virtually all had a quarrel with the church, they seem to have grown beyond anger. My friend Michael, once distanced from the church, said he found great consolation in the liturgy and the community.

Those couples who left the church because the priest balked at baptizing their daughter "Tiffany Kim" might consider slipping into a back pew. These gay Christians cling to their faith even when an Episcopal bishop suggested that St. Paul might have been gay and the church went ballistic.

There was a quiet reverence at this liturgy, reminiscent of earlier Catholic liturgies during which quiet time was allowed. At the homily, the priest repeated the theme that God loves us just as we are. The intentions were announced with great reverence and strong responses. There were no self-serving ones; the gays prayed for all of us—for peace, for joy, for caring.

The *Pater Noster* and kiss of peace were touching moments. People moved around under the beamed ceiling, taking their time to offer peace and friendship. I didn't experience the vague tension frequently felt at those near suburban parishes or the large city churches where an anonymous crowd surrounds us and we feel ourselves to be strangers.

Two religious brothers who devote their lives to a ministry of presence among people with AIDS were in the congregation. Their lives have changed radically since they became involved in this apostolate. They have rearranged the furniture in their souls so completely that both said they could not return to the confined world of selective judgments. "We recognize Christians by how they love, not by how they condemn," Brother Don said.

These Christians helped me to move more freely toward a God

who hears the voices of gay men and women who are living church, not playing church.

I'm going back for a refill.

This tale of a former missionary priest, a former nun and the former proprietor of bordello houses illustrates Tim's conviction that grace is more generously available then many Catholics believe. It also illustrates his abiding interest in the lives of priests and religious after they leave active ministry.

The former priest and the former madam

This is the story of two people with the unlikely names of Hubert Sonnenschein and Odessa Madre. Hubert was a priest; Odessa was a prostitute. It's also a story about "prevenient grace," that divine grace operating in the human will even before it turns to God.

We'll start with the grace-filled life of Hubert Sonnenschein. He was born in Holland 70 years ago. Only a teenager when Hitler invaded Holland, his brother was nearly slaughtered by the Nazis because his surname is one shared with Jews.

Hubert entered the seminary of the White Fathers, now called the Missionaries of Africa, in Boxtel, Holland. In 1951, he was ordained in Jedburgh, Scotland. The society, famous for its flowing white habit and red fez, assigned him to Malawi, a country about the size of Pennsylvania located in Southeast Africa next to Zambia and Tanzania. It is now 19 percent Catholic, thanks to the White Fathers who arrived there in 1889, two years before it became a British protectorate named Nyasaland. It became Malawi in 1964 but suffered under corrupt one-party rule until 1994.

It's a tough place to live; men average only 39 years, women only 41. Only 3 percent of its people are over 65, compared with 48 percent under 15. Seventy-five percent of its nearly 10 million people are illiterate.

It was worse than that when Fr. Sonnenschein arrived more than 40 years ago. He spent 22 years there, 12 of them as pastor of the cathedral in Bembeke, a parish about the size of New Jersey. While pastor, he built at least eight brick outstation churches to replace the mud-sided, grass-roofed ones that were caving in.

He also pressed for a married priesthood in a country where single men are objects of ridicule. "A man was not considered a complete person if he didn't have a wife. He had no authority," Sonnenschein's wife, Mary Anne, recalled years later.

After more than two decades of service, his position on celibacy and other issues such as the treatment of women caused him to be banned from the mission by the bishop. Refused permission to return after his sabbatical, he left his chalice and books at his mission and, after a respite in Holland, went to Los Angeles to do development work for the congregation.

But in the summer of 1973, he resigned from the community, earned a master's degree at Loyola Marymount University and became director of a school for mentally handicapped children in Sunland, California.

While in Africa, he had met Mary Anne, a White Sister from Washington, D.C. "I was only 23 when I first met him," she recalled. "He was on his motorcycle. In those days the only time a nun spoke to a priest was in confession. So I barely knew him."

Mary Anne left her community, too, and returned to Washington. From California, Sonnenschein wrote her a characteristically frank letter and asked, "Do you think we can make it?" They were married in 1974 at St. Paul's Church in Los Angeles.

Hubert served as director of the United Cerebral Palsy Center in Stockton, California. Then he and Mary Anne relocated to Washington to take care of her mother, who had suffered a stroke. Hubert took a job as a translator—he was fluent in eight languages—and later as a math teacher at Gonzaga Prep in the capitol city.

> His theology was as simple as the Our Father. "What would Christ do?" he would ask himself, then plunge ahead.

Hubert and Mary Anne settled in St. Camillus Parish in Silver Spring, Maryland, where they were active as teachers in the catechumenate and in a weekly scripture-sharing class. Hubert also edited a prayer network newsletter and did countless other ministerial tasks that kept his ordination oils glistening for all to see. His theology was as simple as the Our Father. "What would Christ do?" he would ask himself, then plunge ahead.

A bypass operation in 1982 slowed him considerably, however. By 1987, his kidneys failed and he was forced to go on disability and hemodialysis. He had to spend three afternoons each week at a dialysis center near DuPont Circle. It was a debilitating process that sent his blood pressure plunging and left him terribly weak. He was assigned one of those recliner chairs in a large room along with 40 other dialysis patients.

The patient in the next chair was Odessa Madre.

Madre was born in a depressed Washington area known as Cowtown in 1907. Her grandfather had fought in the Union Army in the Civil War. She grew up in a black ghetto that nestled alongside an

Irish Ghetto. It was a time when blacks fought with blacks and Irish with Irish. Somehow segregation kept the two groups from warring with each other.

Madre was smart. She attended Catholic school and by 1925 managed to complete high school. But the Depression soon followed, and Odessa, black and poor, could find no real job. She was driven into prostitution, gambling and, later, drugs.

It's hard to catalog the accomplishments of a madam but, in the years that followed, Odessa became the proprietor of four or five thriving bordellos. (The Irish boys with whom she had been raised had gone on the D.C. police force. They closed their eyes to their friend's employment.)

Odessa succeeded in her world as well as Hubert had in his missionary work. She was bright, colorful, flamboyant. Odessa could often be seen, her 220-pound body swathed in furs, relaxing in the back of her limousine, traveling from one franchise to another. She was as generous as she was colorful, one of the easiest touches in town. Odessa probably gave away as much money as she laundered.

In 1949, Congressman Estes Kefauver of Tennessee became a senator. A year later, he directed a highly publicized investigation into organized crime. He didn't get the big players, but the effort earned him a vice-presidential nomination. His committee snagged Odessa, and she was sent to jail. The Internal Revenue Service took her money to satisfy her tax debts, and while she did her time her friends stripped her of all her other possessions. When she came out of jail she was destitute.

When Odessa's kidneys failed, the Medicaid people got her into dialysis, where her chair was next to Hubert's.

They talked. Odessa was 80 years old by then, emaciated and sometimes delusional. From his years in Malawi, Hubert remembered what hunger looked like and realized that Odessa was slowly starving to death. Medicaid would flush her kidneys, but it couldn't feed her.

Hubert began making sandwiches for Odessa and bringing them to the center. The missionary and the madam became as close as Jesus and the woman at the well.

> The missionary and the madam became as close as Jesus and the woman at the well.

Hubert and Odessa continued treatment for more than two years. By then, complications made it more difficult for him to get to the center. So he mastered the process of self-administered peritoneal dialysis and, for the remaining five years of his life, Hubert performed the task at home.

Before he left the center, however, Hubert organized the other patients in order to make certain that Odessa had adequate food.

Odessa Madre lived only three months after Hubert's departure. The Washington papers wrote her up as a colorful madam and creative moneychanger. Hubert wasn't mentioned.

Hubert continued his teaching in the parish until he could no longer manage the stairs in the old convent that served as an education center. By 1993, he could no longer do self-dialysis, so Mary Anne attached him to the machine each night, removing him just before she went to work in the morning.

His final days were marked by delusions. "He seemed to be living at another level," his wife said. "On different days, he thought he was in Holland, in London or in Rome. He was always concerned that his 'visitors' would get a good meal. He was still mostly concerned about the welfare of other people."

On January 15, 1995, Hubert said, "I want to go home." Later the same day, while his wife played and sang his favorite hymns in Chicewa, one of the Bantu languages of Malawi, Hubert died.

Now, something about prevenient grace, that peculiar gift that makes us pay attention to another's needs. It seems to me that God has permitted the thousands of Hubert Sonnenscheins of this world to hear the different drums that caused them to make changes in their lives. Somehow, Odessa Madre had gotten beyond the pale of an institutional church. Only a marginalized priest like Hubert could have reached her.

Perhaps that is why God has permitted the enormous leakage from the priesthood and sisterhood in order to supply ministers to souls who have wandered far beyond the shadows of official steeples.

In Africa, Hubert would occasionally preside at the funeral of a devout polygamist. The social structures were such and medical care was so scarce that the only way one could get deathbed attention was through the loving hands of a second or third wife. Hubert also spoke out about the dreadful customs to which women were subjected. It got him in hot holy water. But he would only ask himself, "What would Jesus do?" Them he would respond with his heart.

Perhaps that is why resigned priests and religious are so frequently found running federal and state agencies, shelters, hospitals and hospices, teaching—even preaching. It may be why they are now helping their pastors to give missions in the parish and even, quietly for now, administering the last rites in hospitals. It may be why a few preside at the weddings and funerals of souls who cannot fit through the needle's eye of institutional rules.

Odessa Madre is only one soul who was touched by one of the church's marginalized people. "We refused to let the church squeeze us out," Hubert's widow said. "I believe that the Holy Spirit works among the so-called marginalized people. And I think Hubert and myself are among the marginalized."

Mary Anne Sonnenschein was right. But perhaps resigned priests and former religious are no longer marginalized, at least the way they used to be. The needs are too great and the "indelible marks" too visible. The Mary Annes and Huberts somehow never lose the dedication that caused them to prostrate themselves on ordination or habit day.

I've talked with literally hundreds of them. Only one exception comes to mind, although I'm sure there are others. This guy threw his ministry aside and became a successful businessman. I met him not long ago, however. He is 55 and quitting his job. "I think I'll go over to Catholic Charities," he said. "I still have my Spanish. Maybe they can use me."

It all reminds one of the death scene at the close of George Bernanos' *The Diary of a Country Priest*. The dying priest asks an absolution of a man completely unqualified to administer it. "Although I realized that I had no right to accede over-hastily to this request," the fictional Monsieur Dufrety wrote, "it was quite impossible in the name of humanity and friendship to refuse him."

"Does it matter?" the dying priest said. "Grace is everywhere."

Tim discovered that all manner of adjustments are being made in Catholic parishes due to the priest shortage, many of them innovative, even illegal. And he was intrigued, not terrified, by what that may mean in the long run.

A priest in every pot or... a penny for your priest

Angus Tully had been around horses all his life, even back in Catholic Ireland, where the definition of a Protestant was an Irishman with a horse. His religious faith was conceptually akin to his long-dead mother's belief in leprechauns. "Of course, I don't believe in them," she used to whisper. "But they're there."

Angus was nearly 60 before he married. He had spent his life in stables, rodeos, riding academies and the like. It made perfect sense for him that he be married on his horse and under his 10-gallon hat.

"I don't have a 10-gallon hat," Fr. Ambrose Deady, the priest who was to do the wedding ceremony, told me. "But I've talked to the couple. They are decent, hard-working people. They've got trace marks of Catholic blood. There won't be any children and they ask nothing more of the church except to be buried from it."

"I'm not getting up on any horse," Deady continued. "But I'm going to marry them. I'll dress like a Lutheran minister and hope I don't get caught."

I'm hearing more and more stories like that these days. They are part of an evolving church that now must react more and more like Tevya in *Fiddler on the Roof* rather than checking with the office manual.

Another story has a pastor confronted by a couple caught in a canon law jam concerning the man's previous marriage. The pastor advised them to get married by a judge and promised to provide a blessing afterward, largely so the man's devout, aged mother would not be hurt. When the couple arrived without the marriage certificate signed by the judge, the pastor bit his tongue and married them with the mother in mind.

> *Sensitive pastors are being asked to stretch their sacramental garments to cover all manner of situations. It amounts to an underground church.*

Within a week, the chancellor had mailed back what priests sometimes refer to as a "gotcha letter." It contained a copy of the marriage certificate the offending priest had signed. The pastor got his teeth kicked in. The chancellor got promotion points.

But chancery discipline has done little to slow the changing direction of pastoral services in a church that continues to lose business. Sensitive pastors are being asked to stretch their sacramental garments to cover all manner of situations. It amounts to an underground church.

Recently one pastor told me he had presided at mass 11 times during a single weekend. In another case, three clerical jubilarians left a retirement party early because all were presiding at Saturday evening Masses. The youngest of them was 77. Elsewhere an 81-year-old bishop delivered a touching homily at the funeral of an 18-year-old boy. These men's fires have never gone out.

But now take a look at the new liturgy of the Eucharist in the absence of a priest. In one large parish in Eden Prairie, Minnesota, and undoubtedly others, it has completely replaced the weekday mass. In other case it replaces the morning mass on any day when there is a funeral or a wedding.

"I had 77 funerals last year," the nearly 70-year-old pastor said.

> The pastor's solution makes sense, given the worsening priest shortage. But in other cases, changes may be linked to the vagaries of human nature.

"If I'm going to be a good pastor, I've got to visit the dying person. Then I've got to go to the wake, do a service there and then prepare a homily. The next day, I do the funeral and then go to the cemetery and the family luncheon.

"It's almost as bad with weddings, he added. "I had about two dozen of them last year. So I don't have a morning Mass on wedding or funeral days. That's a least one-third of my year."

The pastor's solution makes sense, given the worsening priest shortage. But in other cases, changes may be linked to the vagaries of human nature.

Emerging evidence shows that weekday mass is on the wane partly because some priests are just too lazy to preside. A number of pastoral associates confide that they quietly check out the rectory each morning to ascertain if Father is up. When he is not, they must preside at the absent-priest liturgy. Further, they admit that the priest-less liturgy itself is evolving.

The pastoral associates now process down the aisle and occupy the presider's chair. They let others do the readings, give the homily and recite virtually every prayer except the words of consecration— all while the pastor, who would not have made acolyte back in the days when priests were abundant, is still in bed.

Then there is Manus Boyle, a resigned priest who serves as chaplain at a local public hospital. It's a small hospital hardly worthy of the local parish's attention. (In fairness, some of the bean counters administering hospitals have said that floor nurses are not to call clergy until a patient has expired, short of a specific request. The standard line: "It's not the highest and best use of the priests' skills.")

Manus Boyle makes cold calls on all patients. He finds Catholics who have drifted from the church but want reconciliation before they are delivered home. He always offers the services of a priest but, as often as not, finds souls who have been adrift for too long. So Boyle reasons that he cannot turn away someone in an emergency. He shrives and anoints them and brings them the Eucharist. He'll even officiate at a non-eucharistic liturgy at the funeral home.

Then there's old Leo Crumlish, who never saved a nickel during his years of active ministry. He served at a time when extra income came largely through stipends. He hated being a sacramental jukebox, so he retired on a pension that barely covers his rent and his car.

Leo now supplements his income presiding at burials of souls that are unattached to a church, including many Catholics whose families stopped practicing after Confirmation.

Leo wears something appropriate, does a decent service and shares a piece of the $150 add-on that the funeral director collects for the use of the room, including the rented crucifix and statue of the Blessed Mother. In a good month, Leo can add about $200 to his pension. It enables him to eat Chinese food once a week.

Weddings may cause priests to stretch the most. "If they come to my parish," one pastor said, "I have to assume that they're people of good faith. I'm not a cop. Sometimes their backgrounds are so confusing all I can do is wipe the slate clean and start them all over again."

All this comes at a time when the institutional church acts increasingly like the U.S. Postal Service, with autocratic managers engaging in tactics that only engender more frustration and anger. "I just got a long letter from my bishop," one pastor wrote. "It was two pages on the use of the words *host* versus *bread*. I tossed it in the kitchen trashcan."

This situation comes, too, when seminaries can't recruit the best. It comes when the Dioceses of Altoona-Johnstown, Pennsylvania, announces that it will close 38 of its 138 parishes by 2000; Providence, Rhode Island, announces that it may close or merge 30; Pittsburgh has gone from 323 parishes to 220; Dayton, Ohio, projects only 9 priests for 17 parishes in the inner city. The list simply grows.

Meanwhile, face-to-face reconciliation can take up to nine minutes per soul and U.S. bishops forbid group reconciliation.

Indeed, perhaps the one thing permitting the church to keep its head above water is the fact that fewer Catholics are practicing. Thus, one parish, so large that a priest-friend likens it to an aircraft carrier, has an attendance rate of only 30 percent among its 17,000 parishioners. At Christmas, it takes 17 Masses to handle the backsliders who appear only on those feasts ranked in the *ordo* as "doubles of the first class." But on Sundays, the church manages with only five masses only because a lot of their parishioners are off to the links.

In the tiny diocese of Victoria, British Columbia, Bishop Remi J. DeRoo takes a philosophical view of declining practice. He has been living with that evolving diocese since he was installed in 1962. In 33 years, the percentage of Catholics in Canada's most western province has increased from 10 percent to 18 percent, but the number attending Mass has remained at 10 percent.

DeRoo is unruffled. "Jesus was never a parishioner," he said. "He never intended to found a church."

DeRoo believes that Catholics may be evolving into a community that doesn't need new churches. The most promising Catholics, he finds, don't see themselves as related to a specific parish. He is witnessing the establishment of ecumenical communities not related to parishes or leashed to a chancery desk. In fact, he finds that small Christian communities controlled by priests have a lower survival rate than the freestanding ones.

> DeRoo believes that Catholics may be evolving into a community that doesn't need new churches. The most promising Catholics, he finds, don't see themselves as related to a specific parish.

DeRoo is finding that the majority of those Christians most in need of ministry are no longer in church, but he is saddened by the thought that "at the very moment when institutions are on eve of collapse, they seem bent on reaffirming their power and bringing everything under control and convincing themselves that they can weather the storm.

"We are into a very heavy session of Good Friday," he concluded in a recent address, "and Easter is a long way around the corner."

But Catholics are as tough as weeds growing in sidewalk cracks. "Their faith is up in the attic," one priest said. "They'll go up and get it when they need it."

Almost anything Tim wrote about women in the church was tinged with his simmering indignation over their second-class citizenship and the stained glass ceiling that keeps women in their place. Here he found something to cheer about in the story of the female rector of an Episcopal church in suburban Chicago.

A woman, a priest, a death in the family

Recently, my wife Jean and I went to the local funeral parlor to bid a farewell to the father of a friend. There we found three clerical collars hovering near the coffin, helping the widow and comforting mourners with voices as soft as a baby's behind. All three had been "priested," to use the Episcopal terminology, in recent years. Each wore a black tailored blazer and charcoal-gray skirt. All three were, God forbid, female.

The experience caused me to drive on another day to Flossmoor, Illinois, a lace-curtain Chicago suburb, to visit the Church of St. John the Evangelist and meet its 41-year-old rector, the Reverend Mary Grace Williams. We talked over a meal of Chinese food, a strong preference of Williams since she visited China in 1994 and brought back a 5-month-old baby girl who had been left on a busy street in the forbidden city of Wuhan.

Grace Elizabeth Li Williams only serves to enrich her mother's priesthood. She often rests in her vested mother's arms as she greets worshippers on Sunday. "I'd like to get married someday, but just now I'm too involved with St. John's and my daughter," said Williams, a former Roman Catholic.

Williams is one of only 20-25 ordained Episcopal women who have been named rectors across the United States, and the Church of St. John is a pastoral plum. Just 65 years old, the 800-member congregation called Williams to be its fourth rector after a nation-wide search. An earlier rector at St. John's, who had been ordained a bishop, was opposed to female priests. A Chicago friend and fellow priest had advised her not to apply.

"But I hadn't really applied," she said. "I had simply filed my ré-sumé with a clearinghouse for all applicants and the search commit-tee found me." In Episcopal tradition, parishioners issue the call and local bishop approves—a far cry from the Catholic practice, which can amount to a spoils system. The committee, after reviewing some 200 candidates, called her eight references and interviewed her for three days.

When her appointment was announced a year ago, one worship-per asked for her pledge card back (the woman has since become an ardent supporter); one family left the parish and a few others refused to accept communion from the new rector. But most accepted her with barely a glance up from their Books of Common Prayer. Williams dislikes titles and is trying to get her congregation to simply call her "Mary Grace." Some still address her as "Reverend" or "Pastor."

Williams loosens their rubrical shackles by her quick wit and ex-pressive manners. Asked by one nervous parishioner if the priest is a lesbian, she responded: "Well, I wasn't yesterday and I'm not one today. But I'm not certain about tomorrow." As for why she became a priest, she sometimes responds simply: "I look stunning in black."

The Episcopal Church in the United States has allowed women priests since 1977. Today, about 10 percent of the church's priests are female, although many attest to being snubbed by male colleagues and only a handful have been named rectors.

Today, the church has only about 2.5 million members worldwide, about the same number as the Catholic Church in Chicago. But it has 15,000 priests—proportionately more than 22 times the number of priests we Catholics have. The Episcopal diocese of Chicago, for example, has 330 priests to serve its 47,500 members, one priest for every 144 parishioners, compared to the Chicago archdiocese, where one priest serves an average of 2,200 parishioners. That difference is just one of the reasons Williams became an Episcopalian. "Catholic churches have gotten like filling stations." She said. "They have lost their personal touch."

With dwindling numbers and lower regular attendance, priests of both sexes in the Episcopal Church find themselves serving smaller congregations. Membership has dropped 31 percent in the past 22 years. Still, it counts among its new members many women who, like Williams, have left the Roman Church for a spiritual home in which they could realize a deeply felt calling.

Born in Kansas City, Missouri, Williams completed her undergraduate work at Rutgers in 1976, leaving with a bachelor's degree in theater. During her late teens, she drifted away from the church but eventually found her way back through the Catholic chapel at New York University.

She completed her master's in religious education at Fordham University and was hired as director of religious education at St. Joseph's Catholic Church in lower Manhattan. "But after a while, I began to feel that this wasn't enough," she said. "I loved the work but chafed under the restrictions Catholicism placed on me as a woman. I felt called to be a priest, and I felt trapped when I realized I couldn't be one."

In 1980, she entered the Divinity School of Yale University. "I matriculated with the intention of being ordained," she said. "I didn't know whether it would be as an Episcopal priest or a minister with the United Church of Christ." In 1984, after much soul-searching, she entered the Episcopal Church of St. Luke in the Fields of New York.

She was awarded her master's in divinity in 1988 and was ordained in 1989. Yale's Divinity School, like Harvard's, is 50 percent female. About half of the women are Roman Catholics. They represent a treasure trove of high-level talent that is largely being lost to the Catholic Church. "Whenever he speaks on women, John Paul II is our best evangelizer," according to an Episcopal priest interviewed by Bob McClory for *NCR*.

〰 Yale's Divinity School, like Harvard's, is 50 percent female. About half of the women are Roman Catholics. They represent a treasure trove of high-level talent that is largely being lost to the Catholic Church.

"I think I've got the best of both worlds now," Williams said as we toured her mini-Gothic brick church. "The Episcopal Church is a three-legged footstool of scripture, tradition and reason. It's a church that has room for all to come in to find common ground."

Her job at St. John's isn't an easy one. She averages 10- to 12-hour days and has only recently been given an assistant priest. But the structure permits her to do purely pastoral work. "I don't even know who contributes what," she said. "I don't have to and I don't want to." The vestry (read parish council) runs the church, especially its stewardship program.

As we walked though the church, the priest whispered tasks that she hoped to accomplish but stressed that such decisions were not in her hands. Even as we spoke, George Boggs, the parish treasurer, arrived with a small stack of paychecks, including hers. (Meanwhile, already overworked Catholic pastors are expected to sign all checks and monitor all budgets. Indeed, many spend much of their time in tasks completely removed from priesthood.)

If Williams felt anger when she left the Roman Catholic communion, it has long passed. Now, she views her first spiritual home with sadness. After nearly a year at St. John's, she is only vaguely aware of the hierarchy that forms the infrastructure of her diocese. Her interests are far more relational than political. She simply shakes her head sadly when she hears the bloodless statements of a frightened Vatican bureaucracy—such as the recent one declaring "infallibly" that women may not be priests.

Williams reminds me of the women at the foot of the cross or the door of the tomb. Their voices call out but are not heard...because the men have fled the scene. The St. John's community is blessed to have Mary Grace Williams. For her Roman Catholic brothers and sisters, our loss of her ministry is like a death in the family.

In contrast to his usual light-hearted poking of fun at hierarchical excess, Tim is far more serious in his commentary on Bishop Fabian Bruskewitz who, in effect, excommunicated anyone in his diocese belonging to the Catholic reform group Call to Action and half a dozen other organizations. Tim's question, "What to do with a proverbial loose cannon in a morass of canon law?"

Making even the most bilious bishops look benign

I wasn't going to write anything about the brouhaha ignited by the Most Reverend Fabian W. Bruskewitz, draconian bishop of Lincoln, Nebraska, the Pitcairn Island of the American church. But it may be the most exciting thing that has happened in the U.S. church since the Blessed Mother appeared in a dollop of Paul Newman's salad dressing during a church picnic.

I was satisfied to simply attach my bumper sticker saying, "Free the Lincoln 84,000" and let digestion take its course. I did think about driving by Bruskewitz's chancery on Sheridan Boulevard in Lincoln and squirting Lourdes water on his coat of arms.

But, alas, the event has so energized everyone that I am driven to insightful observations.

Clerical humor, always astute and wonderfully disrespectful, has gotten a booster shot. Bishops have snapped to attention. Canon lawyers have emerged from their lairs. To capitalize on the moment,

Call to Action, the real target of Bruskewitz's flame-throwing crosier, is sending out membership and fundraising literature. The religious media, including *NCR*, is burning up is computer terminals and fax machines. Readers who forget to write their mothers are deluging "Repartee" with letters.

〰️ We became convinced that the Bruskewitz mandate was the greatest thing since canned beer.

"Are other churches as crazy as this?" one priest asked my wife Jean and me as he stood waving his arms in our doorway. He couldn't even wait until we took his coat. "Should I punch out and go to another church?" he asked. "This is nutty!"

Our visiting priest talked some more over dinner. We became convinced that the Bruskewitz mandate was the greatest thing since canned beer. "Hell, it has even boosted Bruskewitz," a resigned priest said. "He must love all the attention."

It could be true. The former parish priest from the Milwaukee archdiocese spoke before 700 old faithfuls at a recent gathering of the Institute of Religious Life, held at the Center for the Development of Ministry at Mundelein, Illinois. (The Institute is not connected with the archdiocese of Chicago. It's closer to Mother Angelica's EWTN or Joseph Fessio's Ignatius Press, two conservative groups. "We book non-Catholic events here," a spokesperson for the center said. "We could hardly turn *them* down.")

The bishop's appearance was not long after he had issued his ultimatum, in which he threatened more people with excommunication than Clement VII did when he busted Henry VIII in 1533.

Allegedly, Bruskewitz got a standing ovation. It was just one of the many ironies connected with the meeting. Chicago's Cardinal Joseph Bernardin had allowed them the use of his seminary property, a courtesy the bishop of Lincoln, who ranks 343 places behind Bernardin in the ecclesiastical pecking order, would never have extended to Bernardin. Yet some speakers at the meeting used it as a chance to pillory the cardinal. Bruskewitz did not excommunicate them.

The Wanderer, in an editorial headlined "Bishop Bruskewitz speaks with the authority of Christ," called Bernardin a "backstabber," while another story in the same issue hosannaed Bruskewitz with a lead proclaiming: "Hurrah! A bishop who governs."

Canon lawyers are rarely seen and only occasionally heard. But Bruskewitz sent them running to consult the church's bylaws. I checked my copy of the green-covered book. "A legislator is not to threaten automatic penalties unless perhaps against certain particularly treacherous offenses," Canon 1318 said in language that even I could understand. And a cluster of other canons in Book Six of the code made it clear that doubtful laws do not apply and that Bruskewitz had little regard for the value of church membership. He would have to go to Iraq to find a canonist who would agree with him.

There's a good chance that the priests of the Lincoln diocese are enjoying a breather while Bruskewitz is blinded by the oncoming locomotive of publicity. The 109-year-old diocese rarely gets noticed. Before Bruskewitz, it was led by Glennon P. Flavin from 1967 until 1992. Flavin was considered conservative until Bruskewitz arrived and drew the Episcopal cincture even tighter. Until he arrived, the diocese's only claim to fame was its ban on female Mass servers, a distinction it shares with Arlington, Virginia.

It's likely, however, that Bruskewitz will now be kinder to his priests for the time being, if only to convince his fellow bishops that he is pastorally sensitive.

Lincoln has 135 parishes, one for each priest. He can hardly suspend anyone. Allowing for the retired, sick and missing in action, it's likely less than 100 of the priests are working full time. Somewhat dated figures—1992—suggest that the bishop may have as many as 48 parishes without a resident pastor. He doesn't have much wiggle room for suspending priests who dare to have female servers.

Fabian Bruskewitz is a Roman. He studied at the North American College and Gregorian University, where James A. Coriden was a fellow student. Now a professor of church law at Washington theological Union, Coriden, writing in *Commonweal*, describes him as "an alert, confident, cheery young man, always genial and good-humored." Now, it seems, he has been holding his cellular phone too close to his brain.

Bruskewitz worked at the Vatican and may have contracted scarlet fever working in the Congregation fro Catholic Education and compiling negative information on his Milwaukee boss, Archbishop Rembert Weakland. His leap from the pastorate of St. Bernard's Parish in Wauwatosa could hardly have been accomplished without some Roman clout. He had to catapult over nearly 100 auxiliary bishops to become an ordinary. Most say that his throne came though Justin Rigali, now archbishop of St. Louis but in 1992 the secretary for the Congregation for Bishops and the College of Cardinals.

Lincoln may be a good starter see for the four-year bishop, although only three of his seven predecessors have gone on to bigger sandboxes.

Not a single bishop has raised his crosier in support of Bruskewitz's pogrom. But they owe him a vote of thanks. Their stock with their own priests rose dramatically. "Geez, are we lucky!" said one. "Our guy has his faults, but he's playing with a full deck." Bruskewitz had made even the most bilious bishops look benign.

But the bishops must also be burning incense without matches over this maverick. The ecclesiastical practice of standing miter to miter has tarred them all with the same brush, making them all objects of ridicule at a time when their influence is already lower than whale droppings. To casually informed Catholics, they all remain frozen in the public eye as if carved in a cathedral entrance.

"It's a bad combination," one Bruskewitz observer said. "Dumb and ambitious."

Bruskewitz may have divined that most of his episcopal brothers have been reduced in status to the level of office managers. The Vatican now makes episcopal appointments, often with little or no local consultation. So he's using his clout there. He needs only to take actions that make him appear magisterial to Vatican bureaucrats wired to John Paul II.

"Not his time," another observer said in a local Catholic bookstore. "He may have overplayed his hand. The Vatican wants guys that are nuanced. This man is a lobster."

Rectory banter rose dramatically after all those Masonic Rainbow Girls were informed that their souls were in jeopardy. Many clerical phone calls started with "This is Bishop Bruskewitz" and the "can-you-top-this?" dialogue was on. It was an emotional physic for a lot of tired people.

"He'll never implement it," one observer said. "What's he gonna do? Install bar codes?"

"Ignorant bishops don't deserve such attention," my friend Tom McMahon wrote from California. "The bishops have forgotten the 'fear not' of Luke" (8:50).

Others were even more angry. "Mother Angelica can say anything she damn pleases," one man observed. "Bruskewitz can bully thousands of people. The bishops won't open their mouths. They're terrified of these two fools."

"But they'll organize to silence Dick McBrien," the man continued. (Fr. Richard P. McBrien, professor of theology at the University of Notre Dame, is under scrutiny for alleged mini-heresies in his book, *Catholicism*.) "It's insane. Thinking people are pulling away."

> Bishops break out in shingles in the face of ambiguity; laity live with it each day in their homes, jobs and social life.

"I'm satisfied to be one of the sheep," a faithful professional woman said. "But I'm not a dumb sheep!" Both Bruskewitz and his fellow bishops continue to use patronizing language when referencing the faithful. They seem to think the sheep are chronically confused and in need of clear-minded celibates who will clear up any ambiguities. Bishops break out in shingles in the face of ambiguity; laity live with it each day in their homes, jobs and social life.

In a memo to his priests, quoted in *NCR*, Bruskewitz also took on what he considered immodestly dressed women and homosexuals. His statements regarding women's dress exposed more of his mindset than it did the women's knees.

What to do with a proverbial loose cannon in a morass of canon law? There was a time when, after a decent interval, such bishops could be promoted to the Vatican and placed in charge of monitoring the beeswax in paschal candles. Presently, however, it is precisely these Queegs who are being appointed to whip the sheep or drive them out. Good shepherds don't need fences; poor ones erect them as fast as they can.

Lincoln nestles against the smaller, even more rural diocese of Grand Island, Nebraska. It is presided over by Bishop Lawrence J. McNamara, a gentle soul who was educated at Chicago's Mundelein Seminary. "All those Lincoln Catholics who are excommunicated," one of McNamara's classmates said, "can just drive over to Grand Island and get communicated again."

Take heart. This is the true church. No other would have survived.

For many years Tim was a prime member of a weekly luncheon group, the only one among them who was not a resigned priest. It was there that he often displayed his considerable talents as a raconteur and it was where he picked up insights, ideas and stories for his columns.

Retired Old Men Eating Out

The Romeos meet most Wednesdays at Gulliver's Restaurant on Howard Street on Chicago's northern border. (Howard is the dividing line between what was once Catholic Chicago, which was wet, and WASP Evanston, which was dry. Evanston is the Vatican of the Woman's Christian Temperance Union. Uncounted numbers of WASPS were martyred trying to cross Howard to secure a drop of the creature from the brown bag stores owned by the papists.)

Gulliver's is wet, but none of the Romeos drink—or smoke—at least not at lunch. Catholics just don't sin like they used to. The Romeos gather around the dark, wooden table under a spectacular collection of antique light fixtures and study the menu, which is only slightly shorter than War and Peace. Reading the pasta section alone can give one gas.

But I digress. Romeos is an acronym, dreamed up by Carole, one of the spouses. It stands for Retired Old Men Eating Out. Most, indeed, are retired and most are enrolled in Medicare—a blessing because if the Red Cross learned of the men's many ailments they would send a sandwich and coffee truck. There is cancer, heart bypass, dialysis, diabetes, fading eyes, prostate problems, hearing problems and so on. Yet, there are no complaints. Instead, they are more concerned with each other's ailments than their own.

All are married. All are practicing Catholics. All are involved in some capacity in their parishes. The group has no charter, no rules, no dues or mailing list. Affiliation with the Romeos won't appear in their obituaries. In a world in which drug cartels have mission statements, the Romeos exist on the thin air of tolerance and the strong bonds of friendship.

Most of the Romeos are resigned priests, although I'm not, and some—especially visiting clergy—are still on a diocesan or congregation roster. Harvey, a retired priest from another diocese, was there recently, for example. He was filling in for a local pastor who was in Ireland. The Romeos were laughing at Harvey's account of his encounter with a woman who had chided him after Mass for his failure to kiss the gospel book at the conclusion of the gospel reading. "Madam, I don't kiss things," Harvey said to her. "I kiss people." Then, he threw his arms around her and thawed her liturgical ice. Romeos love substance laughing at image.

Most of the Romeos left active ministry during the years that followed Vatican II. But they cling to the church like wet leaves and volunteer for everything under the dome. Jim plans liturgies for a university chapel; Marty directs a satellite liturgy in his parish for a group of mostly elderly people, some of whom he drives to a local school of podiatry to have their toenails clipped. Barry, a former juvenile court officer, monitors the case of a good friend's son. Peter is

> Most of the Romeos left active ministry during the years that followed Vatican II. But they cling to the church like wet leaves and volunteer for everything under the dome.

the business manager in his parish. Frank, who lives part of the year in Florida, walks around his seaside parish, inviting stray sheep back into the fold and building the parish roster—this in spite of the fact that his pastor is a former Episcopal priest and a married man. For Frank to be reintegrated into the active priest corps, he would have to abandon his spouse and jump through dozens of hoops. Ed likes intellectual topics. He and his wife run a prayer group out of their home. So it goes.

If I didn't know better, I'd swear they were priests with portfolios.

They gather for occasional days of recollection, and nearly all are part of an annual retreat at a local Benedictine abbey. They pray with the sick and infirm. If I didn't know better, I'd swear they were priests with portfolios.

The Romeos' anger with the church is virtually weightless. They look back with humorous and affectionate nostalgia. I have seen them cry when returning to their seminary for a gathering. (Most are local diocesan priests—a few of over 300 Chicago priests who have resigned—although there is a former Jesuit and a Passionist among them.) At a recent gathering, the group was laughing at an item in a recent issue of *Highlights*, a publication of the Presbyteral Council of the Chicago archdiocese. It contained the news in the chancellor's section about the policy on resigned priests and their roles within the church. "There are theological restrictions about service at the altar (e.g., lector)," the bulletin read. "We are trying to avoid confusion, especially among parishioners and public."

Chancery offices constantly view the faithful as so befuddled that, without unctuous instruction, they would confuse the holy water fountain with a birdbath. "Outreach to a man who is not regularized is important," the bulletin read. "He is probably hurting and may not realize his situation is not impossible." The poor, canonically challenged Romeos enjoyed the patronizing tone. They're not hurting. They've been successful in their jobs. Their lives and marriages are in order. (The divorce rate among resigned priests is only about four percent.) Most are proclaiming the scriptures—even giving occasional homilies—with the blessing of their good friends among the active clergy who are grateful of their talent and assistance. But some canonically driven, active clergy are so prudent that they don't sing "The Star Spangled Banner" without Vatican approval. The newsletter's succinct paragraphs, larded with canonical references, left little room for a pastoral response. The Romeos would prefer an IRS audit.

At the functional level, the Romeos enjoy virtually full acceptance among their fellow clergy and parishioners. They are often the ones who organize class reunions, often held on seminary property with generous support from the local rector. (The silver and golden jubilees are generally hosted by the local bishop, and resigned priests are not invited. But they attend anyway because their still active classmates and friends invite them as part of their ticket quota. No one turns them away.)

The Romeos are an integral part of the clerical gossip network that is common to any healthy organization. If a bishop burps in Podunk, it is heard at Gulliver's faster than e-mail. Most of the rumors are true, especially those heatedly denied by the core administration. Lately, with three U.S. cardinals over retirement age and 20 bishops at or nearing 75, careerist clergy with scarlet fever are piling up frequent flyer miles, attending installations, retirement dinners and funerals where their presence is chronicled by local diocesan papers with platitudinous sentiments intended to pass as episcopal wisdom.

The announcements, together with local appointments, are analyzed by the Romeos for either deserving pastoral gifts or clout, although as the Romeos advance in age their interest in career track clergy turns to amused contempt. Instead, they cheer the efforts of parish clergy whom they meet at wakes and funerals, in hospitals and at the curb before and after Mass.

> There isn't much hope for a church that doesn't listen to its Romeos.

The Romeos are enormously well informed. Jim can provide the name of a bishop of a diocese the size of a lighthouse. They tend to read scripture commentary and thoughtful essays on the future of the church, such as the recent one by retired Archbishop John R. Quinn of San Francisco, *The Reform of the Papacy* (Crossroad, 1999). Books and clippings are shared and commented upon as if Romeos were a priest study group in a diocese. These men could easily slip behind the lectern at a clerical conference and not be spotted until they dropped their wife's shopping list.

Mostly, however, the Romeos tell stories, just as active priests do. The culture of the priesthood is knee deep in clerical lore, some of it dating to the turn of the last century. It is funny and insightful. The rigid, celibate structures of pre-Vatican II life made for enormous pressure on the cassock and biretta corps of priests. But it gave free rein to eccentricities. The result is a body of clerical lore that would sink an ark.

Quinn's book on the reform of the papacy states that if the church is in need of continual reform "she is necessarily in need of continual criticism." There is plenty of that around the Romeos' table at Gulliver's, but the talk is closely linked to John Paul II's own statement about the reform of the papacy. Criticism, the pope wrote, could be a "service of love recognized by all concerned" (*Ut Unum Sint*, 1995).

The dialogue at Gulliver's is not an option but a necessity. There isn't much hope for a church that doesn't listen to its Romeos.

The U.S. census in 2000 got Tim thinking about the old parish census that was an integral part of pre- Vatican church life. And that got him thinking about what would happen if the census was revived today and parishioners were asked what they really think about the church.

Do these questions really matter?

A s a faithful citizen, I have already returned my U.S. Census form to the enumerators who will enter my data into their electronic mailboxes. My nose has been counted as well as our refrigerator, telephone and flush toilet. The data will be stored in a secret place, available only to thousands of bureaucrats until 2072, by which time I will be 143 years old and conceivably won't be offended that my neighbors know that I have a flush toilet.

The U.S. Census has been with us since 1790 when Article I, Section II became part of our Constitution. Its historical ancestry stretches to Jesus' time, which explains how he came to be born in Bethlehem. The census didn't start to ask extra, invasive questions until the 19th century, although race was first asked in 1790. This year, those who got the long form are required to answer 53 questions, the shortest long-form question list since 1940.

I really don't mind too much. After all, the local supermarket already knows what flavor of soup I slurp, and the Barnes & Noble Bookstore monitors virtually every word I read. Never mind what my doctors know about my inner workings. Our local Walgreen's already has my prescriptions on zillions of its computers, and pregnant women report that they get diaper service ads before they return from the obstetrician's office.

However, I do resent the long form's query that asks if anyone in the house "has difficulty learning, remembering or concentrating." My wife Jean now wears a nametag so I know what to call her. I don't want that even mentioned until 2072.

The experience reminds me of the pre-Vatican II days when the parish census was an integral part of church life. It was a time when rectories were stuffed with curates and smelled of the absence of women. Laywomen only ironed corporals, and laymen took up the collection or sold Fr. Coughlin's anti-Semitic *Social Justice* magazine. For the rest, the curates did it all, including the parish census.

> My mother didn't have a lot of faith in life, but she lived a life of faith—and the curate was a symbol of that faith.

At St. Alice's, the arrival of the curate in our home to ask some questions was heralded well in advance. He could have arrived on a donkey and smelled of palms. The only other time the priest arrived was to anoint a poor soul who was en route to the next world. It was a "double of the first class" occasion. My mother didn't have a lot of faith in life, but she lived a life of faith—and the curate was a symbol of that faith.

Chances are, the curate is in his grave now. He blessed the house and put fresh, indulgence-laden water in our Holy Water bottle. We had carefully purchased two beeswax candles, which he blessed and which we put away to be lit during hurricanes. (There must be billions of unburned beeswax candles in this world. We didn't dare use them for anything else except sick calls and hurricanes.) Then the curate would ask the usual questions about whether my parents were married in the church and if the three kids were baptized, had their first Communion and had been confirmed. He must have known all that. After all, I played Frankincense for three years on the Feast of the Epiphany and I could practically say the *Suscipiat* backwards. But he asked all the questions because the census was a serious exercise.

In other homes, he blessed the aged and infirm and the mentally and physically handicapped kids who never left the house. By the time he was finished, the house felt stronger than if it had been built by the third little pig.

Not every census visit went that well. "Mrs. Powell," who lived three doors down, had married a Protestant. Gossip said that the curate had told her that she had to get rid of that man or she would never pass Go. It was hard on my mother because Mr. Powell was a hard-working man. Mrs. Powell never lacked for table money, no small thing in the middle of the Depression.

I'm not sure what parishes did with the census data. Such information is probably used largely for fundraising. Parishes now rely on local Chamber of Commerce data or talk in terms of "high income zip codes" rather than parish data. Today, after decades of narrow theology and rigid law, Catholics have been turned into rebels. A pastor who guards his parish boundaries like a Mob don would only provoke derision.

I wonder what a contemporary parish census would ask: Are you pro-life or pro-choice? Do you favor exclusive language or would your prefer to be excommunicated? Have you ever taken part in a group reconciliation? Do you realize that, according to the Vatican Congregation for Divine Worship and the Sacraments, the latest version of the Psalter is "doctrinally flawed" and "therefore risks being a danger to the faith"? Have you ever chanted a flawed psalm? Do you still call the ambo the pulpit? Do you stand or kneel during the eucharistic prayer? Do you believe that the Mass for Shut-Ins fulfills your Sunday obligation, particularly if it's on Saturday afternoon? If the pastor directs the congregation to gather in the narthex, do you know where the hell he's talking about? Can you sing even one May procession hymn? Have you ever gone to confession by e-mail?

World War II taught us that there were other neighborhoods away from our own. Suburbs grew like shrubs, and every bishop carried a model of a proposed new suburban church in the trunk of his car. The automobile gave Catholics a choice. Some of my devout friends drive at least 30 minutes to a church that welcomes them.

> Lately, Catholics are asking if the questions once asked of them have anything to do with Christ's coming and death on the cross.

Gradually, pastors stopped asking about boundaries and the requirement to be registered in the parish. In fact, it came as news to most of us that canon law had no such requirements.

This census year, citizens are asking if all this data is really necessary. Lately, Catholics are asking if the questions once asked of them have anything to do with Christ's coming and death on the cross. They would ask the church: Why is the law so sacred? Why must not one jot or one tittle of the law be changed?

It seems to me that Catholics are moving away from a button-down theology and a body of laws that are tighter than the top olive in a bottle. It seems to me that they seek love, not the iron collar of prudence and expectation. Yet, the hierarchy still insists on neat piles of dogma, all tied to ecclesiastical consistency.

In my own parish, the pastor's Easter essay cited Nathan Mitchell of the University of Notre Dame. "Jesus showed that the reign of God is not about shutting life out," it said, "but about letting it in—fully, abundantly, exuberantly." I'm becoming convinced that our past obsession with rules and regulations has turned many of us into nonbelievers, something that can happen to anyone who tries to read 10 pages of the new Catechism at one sitting.

Surely, our obsession with sins of the flesh has rendered us sex-obsessed. Sadly, we have become a church that is weak on the strong and strong on the weak. The punitive laws-first system has helped us to create a core administration of too many bishops who have good heads and good hearts, but the two are not connected. We are thus left to deal with the clerical administrator who greets you in his office, which has a coffee table laden with the Code of Canon Law, the Catechism and his doctoral dissertation.

> The punitive laws-first system has helped us to create a core administration of too many bishops who have good heads and good hearts, but the two are not connected.

The great French priest-novelist, Jean Sulivan, who died in 1980, wrote in *Eternity, My Beloved*: "A person is alive only to the extent that she achieves spiritual freedom, radiating the spirit of alleluia, no longer responding to external commands, having become one with God—who never gives an order because He is love."

Archbishop's portable throne heavier than sin
—December 15, 2000

Reminiscing about the elaborate thrones once standard furniture for bishops, allowed Tim to speculate about how old customs gradually disappear, often very slowly. And sometimes when you think the old ways have gone, you discover the church is reviving them again.

One vote for throwing it in the lake if it resurfaces again

Ever since the guy from the chancery called years ago to ask where to bring the archbishop's throne and I declined, I have wondered whatever happened to the elaborate episcopal chair. The archbishop was coming to bless an addition to the school I once administered. The school community wanted a modest, throneless blessing. The archbishop came, sat on a folding chair and didn't seem to mind in the least. I was afraid he would belt me with the holy water bucket.

In technical jargon, a bishop's throne is known as a *cathedra*, a Latin word meaning "chair." By extension, the chair is a symbol of episcopal authority. Thus, a diocesan bishop's church is known as a cathedral because it houses his episcopal chair. When a bishop speaks *ex cathedra*, loyal Catholics are expected to obey or he might use his crosier to break their knees.

Cathedrals still have permanent chairs. Even parishes have scaled-down models for the local nabob. But I wonder often about the long-gone portable throne on which bishops once placed their consecrated bottoms. For me, it represents a symbol of how things change in the church—not with a roar but a whimper.

I never found the now-deceased archbishop's chair. It could be in the basement of the archbishop's mansion or in a seminary attic. One elderly, long-retired priest, who once served as the archbishop's master of ceremonies, recalled that it came in three heavy parts, including the canopy. Its drapes nicely fell into place when the chair was turned upside down and then righted. It was heavier than a mortal sin. Lugging it around would risk herniating Samson before he got his haircut.

For years, the throne was toted by a local department store, owned by a family of the Chosen People (adherents to a "gravely deficient" religion—at least in the view of *Dominus Iesus*, the recent master-religion statement from Cardinal Joseph Ratzinger's bunker). They sometimes moved the throne three times in a single day in order to ensure that it would be in place before His Excellency glided down the nave to jumpstart one liturgy or another.

Some years after the archbishop was installed, he was named a cardinal. The chair was recalled in order to install red upholstery to replace the green. The red would match his watered silk cassock and cape. After that, the department store quietly withdrew, and a retired religious goods salesman, aided by his two sons, lugged the throne around from one confirmation, funeral or dedication to another.

The cardinal died a dozen years later. His successor went to Vatican II and was deeply influenced by the Holy Spirit wafting through the open windows. Gradually, his need for the chair diminished. His successor used it on an optional basis and, well before he died, the throne was consigned to storage.

For me, the throne's history encapsulates how things happen in the church. Customs appear to have a life of their own. Once they reach their apex, they begin to slide—not always directly. It is often three steps forward; two steps back. We appear to be at the two steps back period now. The angels roll back the door of the tomb, and the church rolls the door right back into place. The church just can't take a chance on letting Jesus out. Far better to speak of evil spirits and have exorcists handy to pray over hysterical people. (Just a few years ago, the local exorcist society at the Vatican had 40 members. It now has 400. Chicago has just appointed an exorcist, although it has no record of an exorcism in its history and could likely use a chaplain at a number of the city's psychiatric units.) I have double locked my doors and added six more surge protectors to my hard drive. With all those evil spirits on the loose, one can't take a chance.

The Vatican's recent 36-page announcement on the frequent flyer mileage of each religion and the banning of evil language such as "brother" and "sister" when referring to heretics in other faiths is just another salvo-of-the-month that has been coming from Vatican offices in recent years. Homosexuals have been scourged. Theologians will likely be bar-coded, often by baby bishop theologians who have mail-order degrees in graduate catechism. Couples may soon be required to bring their marriage certificates to mass so that they can receive the Eucharist. Slowly but surely, the bishop's *ex cathedra* throne is moving back onto the church's truck so that he can read the latest papal directive to diminishing numbers of the faithful.

The American church may be drifting toward the now-defunct theology of Cotton Mather (1663-1728), the narrow, intolerant, severe Puritan who wrote over 400 mostly forgotten books centered on evil. He had a strong influence on the Salem Witch Trials in 1692 that sent 19 witches to their deaths. But like most conservative theologies, Puritanism faded along with Jansenism and other reactive teachings. Gradually, as the church dictates even who does the dishes after the Eucharist, it is downloading more and more fundamentalism—enough to raise the "Syllabus of Errors" to the size of an "Encyclopedia of Errors." In the process, the slippage of the faithful will get so bad that the priest shortage will become moot.

Meanwhile, if that throne comes back, I plan to load it on a rented van and toss it in Lake Michigan.

No escape from news of sex scandal, even on a cruise ship
—August 2, 2002

In the midst of the priest abuse scandal, Tim and his wife went on a cruise, allowing him to sort through all the verbiage and draw his own conclusions. He saw this wave of criminal cover-up as one more manifestation of a system long prone to reckless self-protection.

We've got to face the sex abuse scandal straight on

This clerical sex abuse scandal has gotten dirty. My wife Jean and I thought we would get away from it all by taking a cruise, one we had delayed months ago while my bowels growled with cancer. But getting away from the church proved as futile as trying to escape a telemarketer.

The cruise ship had no Catholic chaplain because it was rumored that the shipping company now preferred married men. Just another example of the "ripple" effect of priestly celibacy. We sailed from the white cliffs of Dover, England, as far as St. Petersburg, Russia, and back, visiting countries that were mostly Lutheran. Still, the scandal slithered after us. In London, an Indian priest with a soprano voice and a British accent asked us to pray for "our brother priests" in America. On the ship, a daily digest of *The New York Times* provided a keyhole peep and the latest revelations.

Only in Helsinki, Finland, did we get through a mass, presided over by a Spanish priest—who prayed in Latin, Spanish, English and Finnish—in which we escaped mention of the American church debacle. Boston's Cardinal Bernard Law should move to Finland. There are only 8,000 Catholics and 21 priests in a population of 5,170,000. But the cathedral, not much bigger than some American bishops' vestment cases, was filled for the multilingual Mass. Law could hide there with his lawyers, PR flacks, bodyguards and private pilots.

We came home to a litany of voice mail, some of which invited me to comment on the abuse situation on TV and radio. I can't resist a microphone. I will speak at supermarket openings. Further, I am the beneficiary of *NCR's* courage for the past 17 years in uncovering the church's cover-ups. The local and distant media wanted my thoughts on the ugliest situation since the sale of indulgences was a blue light special.

TV studios resemble the rear ends of computers. They are cluttered with lights and wires. The production crew contrasts sharply with the "talent" (that is, the people who appear on camera) who are all dressed like Brooks Brothers ads and have 60 to 70 teeth, all whiter than the Blessed Mother's. They are all good people, saturated with news pouring in over the Internet. I enjoy just watching them work until someone with a stopwatch wiggles a finger and suddenly I am talking to a cyclops.

Although fairly young, most of the technicians and reporters remember when Bing Crosby and Spencer Tracy were priests. Now, they just can't believe what they're seeing and hearing. It seemed that many were cradle Catholics but were no longer practicing. Much of their alienation had to do with other zero-tolerance issues, especially those having to do with divorce, annulments and second marriages. Too often, marriage tribunals used everything but a rubber hose or kept the petitioner waiting so long they just despaired. Others told tales of petty rules that refused to treat unequal situations unequally or impediments that were smaller than a flea's behind. Now they were following me to the studio plaza, asking: "How do these bishops get away with this stuff? Whose money is it? These guys are accessories to a crime! They want wiggle room. Geez, I'd love to give them some wiggle room! Now my grandchildren aren't even baptized!"

We agreed that it was a Mediterranean (translate Mafia) model, supported by loyalty, secrecy, respect and silence. Although best estimates claimed that at least two-thirds of the bishops had abuse cases in their dioceses, not one has been removed from office. Indeed, you can still sensed recurring anger at the media coming from some bishops. Chicago's Cardinal Francis George likened the press to the Polish communists who had spied on him years ago in Poland. News reporters still experienced coldness and silence when they asked the most innocent questions. Some church lawyers still fought virtually every case, suggesting in some instances that the victims and their families were to blame for the destruction of their own lives. Like good underbosses, the careerist soldiers stuck by their bishops. They didn't want to be found sleeping with the fishes in the bottom of a holy water font. Even bishops who knew that some of their colleagues were accessories to a crime said nothing.

Top bishops face the Vatican, not their people. They administer a cold and largely self-interested institution and are expert at protecting themselves, even at the risk of shredding young peoples' lives. It's likely that the new policies will cost some 2,000 priests and billions of dollars but most unlikely that a single bishop will melt down his episcopal ring to meet the cost. Offending priests will be told that they can no longer wear the clerical collar—a laughable punishment, since the vast majority of the good guys no longer even walk the streets of their parishes with their clerical collar anyway.

The bishops' conference lacks the authority to remove bishops, especially those who drop big envelopes at the Vatican. During a recent executive session, some bishops suggested that some bishops resign, but no names were mentioned. And all that the bishops did decide must be approved by the Vatican, a process that could take two years. Recall that this is the bureaucracy that has forbidden female homilists and the Eucharist to kids who cannot tolerate hosts made of wheat. Now this same bureaucracy looks for solutions to sexual abuse among the redwoods of canon law while abused kids throw up in their bathrooms.

The bishops have apologized. Now they must stop talking and listen with their hearts. They must put their careers on hold and devote themselves to forgiving and seeking healing for their priests. More than anything else they ever do, they must help to heal the wounded victims. Then the people on the cruise, the staffs of the TV stations, NCR subscribers and believing people galore will forgive them.

Late in his career, Tim got around to honoring church ushers, citing their thankless tasks of making room for latecomers, guiding the inebriates, and quieting the chirping cell phones. And he noted how the job is evolving over the years to that of greeter, a position WalMart and other stores have borrowed for efficiency and profit.

Some recognition for those in the back of church

During a recent episode of television's "Everybody Loves Raymond," the foggy protagonist informs his father that he is thinking of returning to the active practice of his faith. Asked what he plans to do when he reenters the state of grace, Raymond announced: "I want to be an usher."

Since Vatican II, the word has fallen into disrepair. They are now called "hospitality ministers" or "greeting facilitators" or some other inflated title much like narthex has replaced vestibule and ambo is the new name for pulpit. In old Anglo-Norman English, usher referred to a doorkeeper. It derived from the Vulgar Latin *ustiarius*. In England, they were often called "beadles," and were regarded as minor church officials.

Beadle is a marvelous word with infinitely more cachet than "protonotary apostolic," a term describing the highest-ranking monsignor. If we hadn't dropped the word beadle, perhaps we wouldn't be in the mess we're in. Beadles not only ushered people to their prepaid pews, but also kept order by whacking people who were noisy or who fell asleep during numbing sermons.

When I was a kid, I used to sell papers outside St. Alice's side door. The Brown brothers had the front door. They had their own *Philadelphia Bulletin* wagon. They were entrepreneurs. I just had a stack of *Bulletins* and a bag of Fr. Charles Coughlin's *Social Justice*, an anti-Semitic screed against Franklin Delano Roosevelt and anyone else concerned with civil liberties. But how was I to know? I only read baseball cards.

I got to know the ushers. They were dressed in their Sunday suits, manning the pew rent tables (10 cents per seat), policing the back of the church, and finding squeeze room in the stuffed pews.

My sainted father was a huge man. Honest pew rent for him would have been 50 cents. But he preferred to stand in back so he could sneak out during the sermon and have a smoke with the ushers. The ushers gathered on the steps, all looking much like the man who comes out when you ring the bell at the meat counter in the supermarket. These men drove trucks and used hammers. One was the local funeral director. Another must have been very old, because one morning, while I served Mass, he sank below the pew in front of him and went to usher heaven. He was bald and had worked in a hardware store, but he read *Social Justice* and I earned two cents from him every week.

Now, over 60 years later, comes Sr. Gretchen Hailer, a Religious of the Sacred Heart of Mary, who has written a user-friendly book for, in her words, "the old guys": *The Joy of Ushers and Hospitality Ministers: Making a Place for Others.*

Hailer is a consultant in adult faith formation. She designs print, video and audio pastoral resources "in order to ease them (ushers and their pastors) into a better understanding of what they may be thinking about." Hailer takes what liturgy people are already doing and tunes it up. She reverences the liturgy but insists that her liturgical recipes be more pastoral than liturgical.

"While genuine welcome is an essential responsibility of the parish doorkeepers," Hailer writes, "it is really only a minor part of their work of service." It isn't easy to usher these days. Uninhibited children now cry at the top of their lungs lest their personalities be stunted. Cell phones bearing powerful messages such as "Bring some bagels home" ring like the hand bells of old. Inebriates and homeless people come for forgiveness or a peanut butter sandwich. Hailer recounts experiences with adolescent ushers with attention deficit disorder and immigrant ushers who unwittingly use obscene gestures to signal a vacant seat. Then, there are those who are unhinged or wanting to listen to their CD player or leave their Rollerblades on.

〰 It isn't easy to usher these days. Uninhibited children now cry at the top of their lungs lest their personalities be stunted. Cell phones bearing powerful messages such as "Bring some bagels home" ring like the hand bells of old.

Hailer lives in Montebello, California. A native of Boston, she joined religious life in 1959. She now writes books and teaches adults in Stockton, Orange, San Francisco and Los Angeles. She freelances elsewhere in the United States, offering days of recollection, retreats and in-service workshops with the hope of revving people up. She is presently researching multiple intelligences. (She also serves on the board of directors of the National Catholic Reporter Publishing Company, although this correspondent has never met her.)

In many ways, she is the typical modern religious—no longer traveling in posses but ministering as a Lone Ranger in order to expand her impact and to find some interior satisfaction. She is now consulting in some Lutheran parishes, without any concern about which faith dimension occupies the corner office. Hailer writes for the 10th-grade level. She is presently doing a book for parish secretaries. Her work seeks affirmation for her subjects. She assumes that they know their liturgy; she only wants to give it some central heating. She isn't writing a *Summa*. One can read her books in the kitchen.

Wal-Mart has borrowed quite successfully from the greeter concept. What's most important is that her ushers and hospitality ministers learn quickly that they are the first experience for the faithful and set a tone for all that is to follow. Gretchen Hailer wants them to understand that they "have unknowingly entertained angels" (Hebrews 13:2).

For Tim the Catholic marriage annulment process was like fresh meat for the lions' cage. It is so prone to manipulation and deceit that he could have written a dozen columns of satire. He didn't. In this one he summed it all up in a few words and carefully noted how some priests are dealing with it.

Annulment, Shmannulment

One of the joys of freelancing is that one generally receives bushels of snail-mail and e-mail, together with voice mail, free books and invitations to speak. Much of the mail is healthy, larded with ideas, good humor and good writing. I am secretly glad that the authors don't write for a living or I'd be peddling Fuller brushes. True, some comes from good souls whose porch light has burned out. However, the mail is as addictive as a holy water font. I enjoy it all.

I have never counted or sorted it all, but a great deal of it has to do with marriage and annulments. It has become easier to dismantle a nuclear weapon than to erase a marriage. Perhaps as few as 10 percent of divorced Catholics even bother to seek an annulment. It is a thorn in their side, an insult to their souls, not unlike a bankruptcy after years of hard work. Marriages, like businesses, start out with the best of intentions.

According to my colleague, John Allen, who heads *NCR's* Rome bureau, annulments went from 600 in 1968 to well over 40,000 in recent years. Americans compose only 6 percent of the world's Catholics but are granted 80 percent of the annulments. In other countries, many diocesan offices don't even have a matrimonial tribunal. The wife gets the house; the husband gets a mistress. The church gets to keep its rigid teaching.

I paused after that thought, and my wife Jean and I went to hear the Chicago Symphony Orchestra play some Franz Liszt. One of the pieces recalled Maria d'Agoult, his former mistress and the mother of his daughter, Cosima. Liszt came from a devoutly Catholic family and took four minor orders for the priesthood under the rigid Pius IX. It reminded me of the great sculptor, Auguste Rodin, who went to daily Mass with his mistress. In Europe, the rules are the same, but the game is played differently. There, Catholics believe in strict rules as long as there is a way around them.

> I checked with my trusty Code of Canon Law and quickly lost count of the laws governing every aspect of marriage except the parts that really count.

As recently as 1970, the church adopted 23 new norms for what is derisively termed "Catholic divorce." The new rules were simpler and more pastoral, but petitioners still faced an invasive and exhausting process. I checked with my trusty Code of Canon Law and quickly lost count of the laws governing every aspect of marriage except the parts that really count. The new *Catechism of the Catholic Church* is also sagging under the weight of finger-wagging prohibitions.

Then, I think of the calls and messages. I'm thinking of "Susan" who married a truckload of beer. After five children, he floated off with her sister-in-law. Following the divorce, the annulment process consumed two years of her time and $800 in fees, while her remarried ex swilled more beer. Her case was slowed by a plodding cleric who seldom did more than one case a week, although he rarely missed a meal or a vacation.

Then "Alex" called because he thought I knew the pope. He's not a Catholic. He was raised a Presbyterian but converted to Judaism when he married Rachel. After 20 years and two children, she took off with a married man. It was a bitter divorce. It took Alex over a year to recover with the aid of a good therapist. Now, he is dating a Roman Catholic, and they want to get married. I tried to find an answer for them. I even called the Marriage Tribunal, but they never called back. (Voice mail has been a boon to church bureaucrats. They can screen every call and decide who is in the state of grace.)

"Cedric" didn't call for help. He just wanted to say that in his diocese the use of the "internal forum" to repair invalid marriages had been virtually banned. The internal forum, used mostly in confession and private annulments, is essentially a moral discernment, usually involving a pastoral advisor, based on the state of conscience of those in a second marriage.

Cedric's call was a dipstick into an increasingly conservative church. Now, given a chance to offer a pastoral or legal response, authorities call their canonist or civil lawyer. In 2001, John Paul II addressed the Roman Rota, the second highest and most active court of the Holy See, which serves as the court of the third instance for most marriage cases and which has been the source of important developments in matrimonial jurisprudence. The pope urged them to avoid loose declarations of nullity based on wiggly interpretations of the provisions, especially those dealing with incapacity of consent.

The call reminded me of a pastoral priest, not an episcopal candidate, who handed a couple an annulment petition and asked them to complete it. The questionnaire permitted them to review their earlier marriage and to reflect on their mistakes in judgment. It was therapeutic. Then, they returned it to the priest who simply stored it in his bureau drawer. Each week he would inquire about their practice and involvement in the parish. Finally, he informed them that their petition had been approved. He married them over the Easter Sunday weekend. The petition never left his underwear drawer.

"They ought to just close the place [marriage tribunal] down," one pastor told me a few years ago. "After eight years of seminary training, if we can't decide such cases, there is something terribly wrong with the system."

With barely enough priests around to staff a Solemn High Mass, we shouldn't be wasting time examining the spoors of bad marriages. It doesn't really heal; it isn't cost effective. It's bad for business. A few in-depth conversations with a sensitive priest or layperson should do the trick.

I am thinking of a couple who wanted to marry. However, there was an impediment that would have taken ages to unravel. So, they went before a judge. However, they knew that his mother would be heartbroken because of the absence of a priest. So, they called on an actor friend and carefully prepared a script. The actor, all vested, carried it off beautifully, and the mother was ecstatic.

The couple lived happily ever after.

Tim gloried in recognizing the achievements of good priests, not the career climbers or publicity seekers but the ones whose lives spoke of honesty and integrity. And he didn't care if they were active priests, laicized priests or married priests. Here he tells of two extraordinary ones.

What priests can be, even without portfolio

R ecently, the Chicago archdiocese lost two of its finest priests. It is a vast diocese, peopled by many good priests who keep their eyes focused on heaven. But Bill Hogan and John Donahue preferred to raise hell on earth.

My wife Jean and I first encountered Hogan when we walked into a peace protest in early Vietnam days. Suddenly, we spotted a man with a microphone in his ear and a camera in his hands. He was taking our picture. We got giddy. But we flattered ourselves. The protester they were after was Hogan, a tall, intense, bearded man who was leading the protest and who likely has an entire drawer at the FBI's Hoover Building in Washington.

We chatted with Hogan as he passed out broadsides protesting the slaughter in Vietnam. We were a trifle nervous about having our picture taken by a trim, suited man with a bulge under his suit coat. However, Hogan seemed overjoyed. Ordained in 1952, he was a curate at Holy Angels, St. Martin de Porres, St. George and Our Lady of Lourdes—all in rapid succession, largely because he got under the birettas and beanies of his pastors and bishops.

His classmate, Bill Flaherty, said at Hogan's funeral that it wasn't easy being his friend, because he made one stretch. Hogan protested against the nuclear arms race and marched with comedian Dick Gregory and the Reverend Jesse Jackson when it would have been more prudent to lead May processions to Mary. He picketed outside Holy Name Cathedral to promote the appointment of black pastors. He reminded others that Catholic parishes in African-American neighborhoods were emptying out, although he showed that, with integration, membership could increase by 300 converts each year.

Hogan marched to integrate the city's beaches. When the Chicago River was dyed green to celebrate St. Patrick's Day, Hogan dumped red dye to protest a bloody war. He was arrested at a Selective Service Office and taken to prison where he promptly began a hunger strike. Finally, the dyspeptic cardinal suspended him and ordered him out of the parish rectory. Some fellow priests took him in. Some time later, the Association of Chicago Priests, an organization of some 500 Chicago priests, petitioned the cardinal, the late John Patrick Cody, and Hogan was reinstated. Further, the association voted to give him its John XXIII Award—its highest honor.

Of course, the honorary vaccination didn't take. Bill continued to live with his widowed mother and at a rectory but drove a taxi at night and worked for a peace coalition by day. Eventually, he faced the issue of celibacy, found it lacking, and married. He became a probation officer. He died on the last day of 2003 and was waked and buried from St. Bride's Parish where he had sung in the choir. His best work was done some years ago, but everyone talked about him for days.

John "Juancho" (it means wide) Donahue was ordained a dozen years after Bill Hogan. Assigned to Visitation Parish, a changing parish presided over by a devout racist, Donahue was soon in hot holy water. Visitation was mixed Latino and African-American, so Donahue went to Puerto Rico to learn Spanish and marched with Martin Luther King, Jr. In 1971, he volunteered for the archdiocese's San Miguelito Mission in Panama, where he lived in a squatters' community without electricity or water. After eight squatter children died because of unsanitary conditions, he organized a group of women who washed their clothes in a public fountain. He was arrested for it.

Donahue returned to Chicago and again to Panama. By this time, he had married Icela "Chelin" ("Little Che") Patino. They would have six children, one of whom died. By 1990, he was back in Chicago where he was hired as the executive director of the Chicago Coalition for the Homeless. He fought for affordable housing, a living wage, health care, the restoration of single room occupancy hotels and a host of other supports that helped keep the homeless off the park benches and out of the airports, train stations and bus terminals. In 2003 alone, the coalition provided 10,000 families with shelter.

> Donahue's wake and funeral were a riot in slow motion. There were 16 priests on the altar at St. Gertrude's Church and more in the congregation.

Donahue did everything with style and courage. Perhaps his most audacious act was to dress a colleague like a tree and take him to the City Council meeting with a sign that read something like: "The city plants thousands of trees, but the homeless have nowhere to live." He could be a thorn in the side of institutions. He had a lot more mileage in him when cancer killed him at 64. His wake and funeral were a riot in slow motion. There were 16 priests on the altar at St. Gertrude's Church and more in the congregation.

Bill Hogan and John Donahue asked a lot of society and the

church. Most of us could only admire from afar—and do a little ourselves.

The demise of limbo was too good a story to be ignored, even if Tim's health was declining. But he did not choose satire. Rather, he seemed a bit sad that this imaginative refuge that once provided a bit of consolation to the bereaved was to be simply swept under the rug. This would be Tim's last column.

Limbo has outlived any usefulness it might have had

When I was a young pimple in grammar school more than 100 pounds ago, we could get a hearty giggle out of the notion of limbo. If a classmate infracted a minor school or social rule, his fellow students would whisper loudly, "Limbo!" It wasn't enough to get one excommunicated, but limbo locked one into heaven's waiting room, banned from the Beatific Vision, unable to pass Go or collect $200.

Frankly, I thought of limbo as a rather special place, free of peer pressure, unlinked to the blessed on the school honor roll—just a quiet, blissful state filled with Hershey bars and free from all those bobbleheads who always remembered to bring their school ties and never lusted after anything other than Uneeda Biscuits.

Formal limbo is said to date to 1378, although Augustine, who died in 430, and Aquinas, who died in 1274, both preached limbo as an abode of the unbaptized where the righteous lived before the coming of Christ. It was a region of conditional oblivion or neglect—a place of confinement, the ablative of *limbus* (a border or a hem), located on the outer turrets of hell. It was kind of like a parking space that forbade parking.

The British monk Pelagius was excommunicated in 417 for denying the existence of original sin and, by extension, limbo. In contrast, Augustine, and to a lesser extent, Aquinas, taught that all who died unbaptized, being in original sin, suffered some degree of positive punishment, largely the absence of the Beatific Vision. Pelagius was catalogued as a heretic while Augustine and Aquinas were awarded doctorates, and I was condemned to memorize some catechism answers that are about to be officially voided.

My old revised *Baltimore Catechism II* cuddles on my bookshelves next to the latest edition of the *Catechism of the Catholic Church*, an overweight volume of 2,865 paragraphs that reads like an IRS handbook. Sadly, limbo is not even mentioned. (There should be a small library of former catechism answers that pre-senile Catholics can de-memorize.)

Now along comes Cardinal Joseph Ratzinger, former archbishop of Munich-Freising, prefect of the Sacred Congregation of the Doctrine of the Faith, vice dean of the College of Cardinals and a member of at least a half-dozen of its commissions, who becomes Pope Benedict XVI. The new pope once thought that limbo was reserved for only the good unbaptized, such as Abraham, Moses, David, John the Baptist, St. Joseph and many others who died before Jesus did. Now, however, Benedict appears to want to fine-tune limbo a bit. He has convened a 30-member papal commission that is likely to consign limbo to just another couplet in Dante's *Purgatorio*.

Not long before he died, John Paul II expanded the decline of limbo by asking a theological commission to consider the question of unbaptized babies. That gesture was a quantum leap from Pius X's 1905 position, which held that the unbaptized did not enjoy God but didn't suffer either. Within another year, it's likely that we will all be told that the two or three limbo responses in my *Baltimore II* have been scratched. Benedict will say that official church teaching never pronounced either way on the existence of limbo and that no official teaching ever advocated the notion. We are all to be left limbo-less.

Limbo once occupied a firm niche in the religious imagination. Now it is on the brink of being reduced to an invented symbol that can readily be left behind. The notion of limbo generates obvious pastoral difficulties, especially those touching on the deaths of infants. Now, especially in Third World countries, infants die by the millions from easily treatable diseases and from AIDS. By the end of 2001, 40 million people had been diagnosed with HIV, 95 percent of them living in developing countries. If limbo were still a reality, there would not be enough room there to swing a cat.

Benedict XVI has given his theologians about a year to announce some new wordings that will get the church out of the corner it has painted itself into. Maybe the Vatican will limit limbo's enrollment simply to the just who lived in pre-Ascension times. I dunno. But after over 65 years, my knuckles are still hurting from Sr. Magella's blows with her clicker because I couldn't remember that limbo was a place of rest and natural happiness.

It's time to widen the doors of the place so we can enjoy the other mansions.

This is an excerpt from Tom Roberts' column announcing Tim's retirement. It quotes Tim's resignation letter, which was vintage Tim and showed how appreciative he was of the opportunity afforded him by the National Catholic Reporter over all the years.

Retiring in true Unsworth style

Several weeks ago I received a letter from longtime *NCR* columnist Tim Unsworth in which he said: "After much muddled reflection, I have concluded that it's time to stick my quill back into the goose and retire from *NCR*."

On one level, it came as no surprise. The many *NCR* readers who have found sustenance and inspiration in his sometimes searing and other times deeply sympathetic depictions of the community called Catholic, or who have frequently smiled and even laughed out loud at his sacred irreverence have noticed he's not been in our pages very often of late.

In recent years he has pushed through a range of medical problems but says as he approaches 77, "My health is deteriorating rapidly."

In true Unsworth style, of course, the news of his deterioration comes packaged in lines that make you want to cry and laugh simultaneously. "And now, a recent MRI shows brain shrinkage. We're testing to see what it means. I am now devouring Aricept, a tiny pill that is virtually guaranteed to unmuddle my brain, which a $2,600 MRI revealed resembles an archipelago of abandoned Pacific islands.

"The final opinion is not yet in and there is much hope. However, those little pills in the bathroom—a salesman's sample—remind me constantly that my brain is becoming a scrambled egg."

Well, not quite. I spent the better part of a day recently with Tim and his wife, Jean, an accomplished artist, in their home, which doubles as a fascinating gallery of painting, collage and sculpture, including her own and pieces from the far corners of the earth. I am no medical expert, but I can tell you that Tim, though noticeably frail, remains a raconteur of the first order, with wonderful news and stories from long ago, from yesterday and all points in between.

"These 24 years," Tim wrote in his resignation letter, "have been most rewarding. They prompted a half-dozen books, dozens of TV appearances, articles in other publications and talks galore.... Above all, my *NCR* link introduced me to extraordinary people, from those still panting from picket lines to those who ringed the pope at audiences. I met enough good people to exhaust all the loaves and fishes without leftovers."

He concluded: "At Mass each Sunday I hear the Gospel proclaimed. During the week, *NCR* arrives and I learn how it is being lived out. May this continue."

I told Tim and Jean that once this news was out they could expect to be the beneficiaries of prayers from far and wide. Feel free to e-mail him and Jean at unsworth3150@comcast.net.

Acknowledgments

There is a lifetime of connections with family, friends, colleagues, students; with all those who have helped me in my career and my life; and with those who are so kind to me in my present state. It makes a long list, so I am bound to forget many, especially in my present state of mental acuity (or lack thereof). So, with profound apologies to those who are not named, I want to thank the following people:

First of all, Jean. My best friend and the love of my life.

Jean's and my families, our deceased parents, my brother Bob Unsworth, his wife Peg and his three children and their spouses; Jean's sister Dolores Rapoport, her husband Ed and her five and his three children and their families, Jean's brother Ken, his wife Kathy and their son and his wife.

The Christian Brothers of Ireland, with whom I spent almost 25 years. Especially my faithful friends Ken Chapman, Donald Paul Dwyer, and Ron Lasik.

Marty Hegarty, his wife Carol, and all of the Romeos ("Retired Old Men Eating Out") with whom I spent many memorable Wednesday lunches at Gulliver's.

The *National Catholic Reporter*—"my paper" for twenty-four years, and especially Tom Fox, Michael Farrell, Tom Roberts, the rest of the staff, who believed in me and welcomed my musings all these years.

Close friends who have stayed with me through my present trauma—Jim Marque, Jack O'Keefe, Jim Lalley, Frank and Joan Tobin, Marilyn Thibeau and her children, John Fahey, John and Jeanne Ann Sattler, Karen Sims and Malachy Walsh, Matthew Cook, Maria Leonard, Roberta Edwards, Stephanie Banta, Harriet and Martin Marty, and Bob and Margaret McClory.

The nurses, CNAs and the rest of the staff of Alden Lincoln Park Rehab, under whose excellent care I am spending my days and nights.

Tom Roberts, who contributed the Foreword, and Bob McClory, who chose the articles in this book and wrote the prefaces to each.

Greg Pierce, whose support and friendship has been there from the beginning and has culminated in the publication of this book.

And finally, I want to thank all my readers. Your letters and emails over the years have meant so much to me. You are part of the communion of saints that is transforming this world, and we will meet again in the next. Thank you all.

Tim Unsworth
Chicago, Illinois
April 18, 2008

OTHER BOOKS FROM THE CHURCH IN CHICAGO

Church, Chicago-style. William Droel celebrates the history of active leadership and lay involvement in the Catholic Church in Chicago. Includes profiles and excerpts from the writing of Russell Barta, Msgr. John Egan, Ed Marciniak, Msgr. George Higgins and others. 126-page paperback, $12.95

The Mass Is Never Ended: Rediscovering Our Mission to Transform the World. Gregory Pierce gives his best argument for taking the Dismissal from Mass seriously and ties it to our mission to transform the world. 126-page paperback, $10.95

Running into the Arms of God: Stories of Prayer/Prayer as Story. Father Patrick Hannon, CSC, uses the liturgical hours as a frame on which to hang twenty-one stories of prayer in the ordinary events of daily life. 128-page hardcover, $15.95; paperback, $11.95

The Geography of God's Mercy: Stories of Compassion and Forgiveness. Father Patrick Hannon, CSC, dives into the common experiences of life and surfaces with nuggets of spiritual gold that reveal the countless ways God shows unconditional love. 160-page hardcover, $17.95; paperback, $12.95

Spirituality at Work: Ten Ways to Balance Your Life On-the-Job. Gregory Pierce offers ten "disciplines" that can be practiced in virtually every workplace to raise your awareness of the presence of God and to allow that awareness to change how you do your work. 160-page paperback, $14.95

Jesus and His Message: An Introduction to the Good News. Legendary Chicago pastor and missionary to Panama Father Leo Mahon provides a clear picture of Jesus and the times in which he lived and the "kingdom" or "reign" of God that he preached. 110-page paperback, $6.95

Gospel Food for Hungry Christians: Matthew, Mark, Luke, John. Theologian John Shea covers the essence of each of the four Gospels in this popular audio series. Six 60-90 minute compact discs in each of the four separate programs, $29.95 each

Available from Booksellers or call 800-397-2282
www.actapublications.com